FROM THE AUTHOR
OF *THE IMPOSTOR
SYNDROME*

EM-PA-THY

THE HUMAN SIDE
OF LEADERSHIP

Harold Hillman PhD

BATEMAN
BOOKS

Published in 2021 by David Bateman Ltd
Unit 2/5 Workspace Drive, Hobsonville, Auckland 0618, New Zealand
www.batemanbooks.co.nz

ISBN 978-1-98-853879-2

Book design: Cheryl Smith, Macarn Design
Printed in China by Toppan Leefung Printing Ltd

CONTENTS

DEDICATION

The *essence* of human connection is probably the best way to describe empathy. It is literally the ability to put yourself in another person's shoes to understand why they think and feel the way they do. It is about being mindful, fully present, suspending judgement and listening with the intent to learn, absorb and give. Empathy is truly about being there.

In our fast-paced world with distractions coming in at us from every direction, it is important to be more purposeful about 'connection' — both at work and at home. Some people have a more intimate connection with their mobile phone than they do with the people around them. Attention spans are limited to the next beep, often at the expense of an important conversation that needs to be had. We will have to work harder over the coming decade to ensure that empathy does not take a back seat to expedience. Empathy loads on quality, not quantity. You can sometimes spend hours with another person, but not really be there with them. And there are times when a deep five-minute conversation with a friend helps to turn their world around.

I dedicate this book to the brave adventurers who, nearly three decades ago, started down the path now known as EQ (emotional quotient, otherwise known as emotional intelligence). There were plenty of sceptics back then who gave little merit to the value we might derive from exploring the less rational, more emotive side of human connection. Thanks to an abundance of compelling evidence, that early scepticism has been replaced by a genuine appreciation for what it means to lead from the heart.

Perhaps the biggest lesson of all from the COVID-19 pandemic is that we often consciously underplay the importance of social connection, taking it for granted more than we ever cared to think. First hand and at a very personal level, we all learned that you only appreciate how important something truly is when it is taken away from you. Living in lockdown opened our eyes to the reality that we are social creatures who need each other in meaningful ways.

My vision for this book is to make empathy real, and to make it right, for leaders who believe that connection truly matters. For every reader, I hope you find a few pearls of wisdom in these pages that will enable you to live and lead with stronger purpose and greater impact.

Harold Hillman
January 2021

ABOUT THE AUTHOR

Harold Hillman is the managing director of Sigmoid Curve Consulting Group. Based in Auckland since 2003 and a New Zealand citizen since 2008, Hillman is a coach to business leaders and executive teams who want to be more purposeful about their leadership and to inspire others to have greater impact with their lives.

Prior to launching Sigmoid, Hillman served in senior executive roles with Fonterra, Prudential Financial and Amoco Corporation. A clinical psychologist in his early career, he developed a passion for leadership development while teaching at the United States Air Force Academy. Hillman was a member of the task force commissioned by the Clinton administration in 1993 to end discrimination against gay citizens wanting to serve openly in the US military.

Hillman earned a master's degree in education from Harvard University and a PhD in clinical psychology from the University of Pittsburgh. His first book, *The Impostor Syndrome*, was published in 2013 and named Whitcoulls Business Book of the Year. His second book, *Fitting In, Standing Out*, was published in 2015. That same year, Hillman delivered a TEDx Talk, 'Inside the Tent', which highlighted his own experience as a closeted gay military officer. Hillman has also co-authored two leadership books with Alex Waddell.

A big fan of learning curves, Hillman will continue to explore the frontier of emotional intelligence over the next decade, pushing forward into new territory to further unleash the power of human potential.

ACKNOWLEDGEMENTS

In a pandemic year when family and human connection have meant so much, I would like to acknowledge:

1. Milton, Alvin and Renae — my two older brothers and younger sister. For the first time ever, we connected on a Zoom call in October 2020. The connection was magical and personified a strong family ethos among us, shaped by our parents, one that reinforces unconditional love and support. I thank you for always backing me and especially for checking on me often during the pandemic.

2. Leslie Renae and Alexis Joy — my daughters, who I often describe as a beautiful confluence of Jackie Kennedy and Michelle Obama. Your mother passed away in January 2020, pre-COVID. At Kim's memorial service, you were both strong exemplars of her dignity, poise and grace. COVID-19 hit hard before you had a proper chance to grieve. Thanks to you both for who you are and for that awesomely delicious birthday cake delivered to my door during Auckland's second lockdown.

3. Churchill and Dean — my two grandsons. The worst thing about 2020 was not being able to see you in person. I especially missed the hugs. You made me LOL numerous times on virtual calls during our respective lockdowns in Auckland and Los Angeles. Kudos to Churchill for winning the 'biggest afro' contest in competition with his

65-year-old Poppie. I must admit I got a slight trim twice during the contest, just so that my clients would not mistake me for Jimi Hendrix. Neither of you will know that name, so do a Google search and check out the brother's afro.

4. Alex Waddell — my best friend and business partner. Your high bar for quality service has distinguished Sigmoid as a respected global brand in the leadership arena. You personify compassionate empathy, the only person I have ever known to perform CPR on a bird — which you revived!

5. Sarah Thornton, my friend and publicist, who has helped me get three books across the finish line since 2013, including a fantastic new partnership with Bateman Books. Thanks also to my friend, Kathleen Lonergan, who is masterful with design and production.

6. Finally, Dame Fran Wilde — a HUGE thanks for writing the foreword. In 1986, your voice was instrumental in overturning the law that rendered 'being a gay man' a criminal offense in New Zealand, a nation that was then ready to distance itself from intolerance and discrimination. You take very little of the credit, while many believe you deserve the most, for making it easier for people like me to be whole. You magnify the true essence of what this book is all about. I am honoured to be your friend.

FOREWORD BY DAME FRAN WILDE

The time for a formal analysis of empathy in the business world has never been more appropriate. In this book Harold Hillman continues the exploration of what makes great leaders, begun in his previous books *The Impostor Syndrome* and *Fitting In, Standing Out*. EM-PA-THY brings together the concepts of aspiration, integrity and authenticity explored in the previous works and focuses these attributes and others on the concept of social connection and its impact in the workplace.

In his introduction, Harold says his vision for the book is to 'make empathy real, and to make it right, for leaders who believe that connection truly matters'. More than any other global catastrophe, the COVID-19 pandemic has brought into full view the need for leaders at all levels to display empathy and to understand that getting under the skin of the others in their team — whether it be a small business or a large country — will help them make decisions that will enhance outcomes for all.

This book focuses on 'how' decisions are made, rather than the classic 'what'. It is based on the idea of EQ, which surfaced nearly 20 years ago, but which, unfortunately, has subsequently often been honoured more as an item of intellectual curiosity than as a key leadership tool. Although the word empathy is widely used (and, as Harold points out, regularly appears in lists of company values), I suspect it is less well understood — much less utilised as a conscious practice in terms of its true meaning and efficacy in building great teams.

The book takes the reader through definitions and illustrations, quoting great thinkers as far back as Aristotle. It includes lay translations of the neural science that underpins human emotions and subsequent behaviour and, most importantly, provides a range of examples that could be taken from many modern enterprises, large and small. These vignettes, drawn from Harold's wide experience in corporate life, his own personal journey and his experience as a mentor and coach, illustrate his model and show how 'an empathetic workplace equals an engaged workforce, and that consistently translates to business success'.

Can empathy be learned? Or is Harold's primer simply a waste of time? Reading this book with its useful case studies indicated to me that consciously developing empathy is very much possible. There are wider examples that support this. For example, in Denmark they teach empathy in schools. All children from age six till they leave school have this behavioural trait as the focus of weekly lessons and are able to exercise and translate into real-world situations what it actually means. The Norwegians also have classes focusing on empathy and other areas of what they regard as basic civil responsibility. It's easy for others from less collectively based cultures to snigger at this as self-righteous state propaganda. But the real question is 'does it work?' Indicators available suggest that absolutely it does. The Nordic countries are consistently voted among the happiest countries in the world. They also consistently lead in other areas.

Recent events in the US have not only highlighted the necessity for empathetic leaders but have demonstrated the tragic consequences of narcissism infecting a political system. The world can learn from countries that objectively endeavour to give young people the ability to steer their populations away from such behaviours.

While changing school curricula as a contribution to shaping a nation's culture may be beyond our individual ability, business leaders can modify the way they relate to others in the workplace, regardless of reporting lines. This book is a vital guide that will greatly assist leaders to analyse and change their own behaviour and impact positively on the culture of their organisations.

Dame Fran Wilde
Business Leader, Former MP, Cabinet Minister and Mayor of Wellington

1

THE OTHER SIDE
OF WHOLE

My life has been an adventure of two halves that have brought me 'full circle' in my quest to be a better man. Full circle implies a concentric journey across time. In my case, that journey has included a wide array of rich experiences across six decades, which have culminated in my life story — one that is infused with a wonderful sense of irony.

I use the word *irony* with purpose here. Among its many definitions, irony was once a literary technique used in Greek tragedies, by which the full significance of a character's words and actions is clear to the audience, although unknown to the character themselves. While I wouldn't necessarily describe my life as a Greek tragedy, the description of the main character living an alternate reality does capture the essence of how I once thought my life might play itself out. So many people waited patiently for me to eventually find myself — the person they already knew. Full circle has a way of making things come right.

The first half of my life was about coming of age in America at a time when being black and gay were both impediments to a fair shot at the American dream. Both required a resolve and resilience to push through social barriers and overt prejudice. I knew I was gay when I was a teenager, but that world and its challenges seemed a million miles away from the more immediate struggles of growing up black and poor in the tumultuous 1960s. I was 12-years-old when Dr Martin Luther King was assassinated. Washington DC and 10 other cities across America went up in flames that night. That was when, for the first time in my life, I realised that race was going to be a very 'real thing' for me. In my short lifetime, our tribe had evolved from being *negroes* to *coloured people* to *black people* and then, there I was — a young *African-American*. Those two words, when hyphenated together, implied something deeper than hue.

I made the choice to park the whole gay side of things. And I chose to impersonate a straight man until I was 40, not realising how detrimental that choice would be to the very fabric of my soul.

So, I made a choice. I chose to get my 'black' on. My focus was on being black, not on being gay. I decided that bearing two crosses simultaneously was too heavy a burden for an introverted teenager who preferred to remain out of the spotlight. I couldn't hide being black, but I could certainly hide being gay, or so I thought. Mind you, I wasn't literate about irony or Greek tragedy at the time. But I made the choice to park the whole gay side of things. And I chose to impersonate a straight man until I was 40, not realising how detrimental that choice would be to the very fabric of my soul.

The second half of my life entails a powerful discovery of self, a reckoning brought about by my service as a military officer, when I was selected to serve on President Clinton's 1993 commission to determine if gay citizens could serve openly in the US armed forces. The end result of that commission was a resounding NO. That gripping experience was the catalyst for me to tackle my own homophobia and embark on the path to becoming a whole person. Even after coming out, my old closet provided safe refuge from a few poignant moments after I joined corporate America, which made me an early sceptic of 'tick the box' diversity.

Fonterra would eventually lead me to New Zealand, a small nation that has taught me some huge lessons about the true power of authenticity and why it is so important in life. I have become a whole person in New Zealand. And, yet, I never would have anticipated that my awakening would find me here. After all, I had unplugged from America, a very proud nation that takes its own perspectives for granted and as givens — in ways that I couldn't fully appreciate until I stepped far enough away to experience the myopia first hand. During my interview with Fonterra, one of the execs described New Zealand as the 'last bus stop on the planet' in terms of its remoteness. Well, that remoteness has done wonders in helping to open my eyes, and my heart, to new ways of thinking about our very diverse world.

I find Kiwis to be far more relaxed around things that are 'lines in the sand' for many Americans — especially when it comes to politics and religion. Across America's conservative heartland, there are people who believe, even if subliminally, that God is a white, gun toting, conservative male who inherently favours America. I would even go so far as to propose that some Americans internalise God as an American. In that world of sharp polarities, who you worship not only determines who you vote for, but also whether you even dare to strike up a conversation with your neighbour.

Living in New Zealand has chilled me out around some of those same mental models that once blocked connection. Twenty years ago, I could never have envisioned that my social network would today consist largely of people who are agnostic or choose not to believe in a God. Today as a Kiwi, I am particularly proud to wear that reality as a virtue. My God makes it possible for everyone to be whole. From where I stand, New Zealand wears its spirituality in a beautiful way.

For me, becoming a whole person has been the culmination of all these things and more. It was ultimately about getting to a time and place in my life when I could smile lovingly at the man in the mirror and accept him fully, without judgement. I spent the first half of my life trying to cover up my blemishes of human imperfection. Prior to coming out, I set a bar for myself that was unreasonable because it was unachievable. I rarely said kind things to myself. I treated my inner persona like a hostage in solitary confinement. I danced around vulnerability, much like how an experienced boxer weaves around his opponent, not fully appreciating that its strategy was to wait me out and to wear me down.

When I least expected it, vulnerability got me on the ropes and clobbered the crap out of me. That knock-out punch was more profound than I ever anticipated. I never even saw it coming. When I regained consciousness, I was far less focused on the pain and much more focused on living life with a deeper sense of purpose. I may have lost the fight, but I found my personal WHY in that battle, which was a huge victory and win for me. I realised that pain is an important part of growth. I had lived enough life to realise that there is some wisdom gained on the other side of any obstacle. I learned to reframe obstacles as a way to learn more about myself. The profound meaning is in the bigger picture. As you grow older, your encounters with obstacles truly do roll up into wisdom and perspective. Among many, this is one of the benefits of having grey hair.

I believe that I earned the street creds to write a book about impostor syndrome, having lived a good deal of my life behind a mask. There is awesome power in unleashing your authentic self, and in making it easier for people who work and live with you to do the same. When my goal was to be the perfect son, husband, father and officer, there was little room for human error in my life. The downside of perfectionism is that you project an energy that says to other people: *Your help is optional.* If you make very little space in your life for imperfection, it is terribly difficult for people around you to offer their support. When you wear vulnerability as a vice, the energy is disconnecting. When you wear it as a virtue, the energy is compelling. It connects you to others because they believe that you really need them for something. For most people, being needed by others is part of living a full life.

On the other side of whole, my WHY resonates with me each and every day. Since claiming New Zealand as home, my sense of purpose has come into even sharper focus. I love where my life's experiences have led me, now actively living out the second half of a story that will undoubtedly see a few more concentric swirls. I am committed to the path I am on, one paved with stones shaped from my own personal WHY, described in these nine words: *To help people lead and live healthier, happier lives.*

Those nine words are why I live as I live and choose as I choose. I love how coming full circle happened for me on the other side of whole. The very best side of whole.

2

EQ: THE NEW BLACK

The Catalyst. In 1995, Daniel Goleman published his now famous book, *Emotional Intelligence*. To be clear, EQ wasn't a new construct then; researchers had been studying and debating its validity since 1964. But Goleman's book was the first to ignite widespread interest and debate over his premise that not only is EQ a real and valid thing, but it would also actually prove to be more important than IQ in determining a person's overall success in life. Goleman went on to propose that, unlike IQ, emotional intelligence is indeed malleable. These bold claims, on a topic that very few people knew anything about, generated a lot of curiosity, especially in the business world.

I was still relatively new to the corporate world then, responsible for management training at Amoco Corporation. I asked a predominantly male audience of senior managers what they thought about this new book on EQ. Their scepticism, even cynicism, was palpable, even though most had not read the book. It was a gut reaction to what many of them considered to be another passing fad that could easily be relegated as 'soft stuff', along with the likes of diversity, inclusion and pretty much anything having to do with the 'touchy feely' side of things. For senior managers in that day, many would have walked barefoot across a sea of shattered glass rather than deal with emotions — their own or anyone else's.

Steady as She Goes. Management was still very much the prevalent paradigm in business when Goleman hit us with this notion that intelligence might be broader than traditional book smarts. Back then, young professionals joined companies and then aspired to move quickly through the management ranks — first as a team manager, then up to functional and division manager, topped off by becoming a general or senior manager in larger organisations. A good manager ensured that the team followed all the sanctioned processes and used the right systems, all in sync with approved protocols and procedures — the standard 'checklist' of things that were considered the essential 'hardware' required to run a business. There was nothing 'touchy feely' about the hardware.

That was a world where loads of hierarchy and formality prevailed, probably best exemplified by the humorous cliché of 'checkers checking checkers', which implied a basic lack of trust and empowerment. As Charles Handy pointed out in his classic work, *The Age of Paradox*, cycles of change ebbed and flowed roughly every 7–10 years back then. 'Steady as she goes' was the preferred way of moving the business forward. It was considered a compliment back then for your manager to describe you as a 'safe pair of hands', which meant that you were unlikely to disturb the peace. Today, that same tag is used to describe someone who has plateaued in their career.

Change was not a relentless constant then, but rather the exception. You truly had time to nail down the status quo and leave it intact for years. Being a good manager was about delivering on your accountabilities. People were promoted based mainly on WHAT they delivered, even if they left dozens of bodies in their wake. HOW they delivered was mostly optional, considered lip service, all part of the 'soft stuff'. I remember that world vividly in my time with Prudential Financial in the aggressive Wall Street culture where your HOW was tantamount to 'whatever it takes to land the deal'. The famous movie *The Wolf of Wall Street* tells the story well.

From Managing to Leading. Fast forward a couple of decades and the leadership paradigm has now taken a strong hold over how we run businesses. It is indeed a new era, one where companies are investing big dollars in developing the best leaders. This is not to marginalise the importance of strong management skills, but the shift in mindset has made it abundantly clear that 'managing' and 'leading' are not one and the same. They are, indeed, two different mental models that produce different skillsets and outcomes. To that end, the shift has been purposeful and with clear impact.

Bolstered by an increased focus on employee and customer engagement, the benefits of EQ in business have become very evident. Under the old management realm, the prevailing assumption was that employee satisfaction was largely driven by decent salaries, benefits and retirement plans; the subtle inference being: 'Aren't you lucky to work here?' That mindset has shifted dramatically, especially with the advent of millennials and Gen Z, along with their prevalent mentality: 'Aren't you lucky to have me?'

You can track the shift from managing to leading in the language now being used by team leaders at all levels. Words such as *vision, values, empowerment, inspiration, aspiration, engagement, authenticity, collaboration, inclusion, wellbeing* — these have become pretty standard in conversations with chief executives and senior leaders in organisations who understand the arsenal required in the very real 'war for talent'. To attract and retain the best people, they now understand that their HOW is as important, if not more so, than their WHAT. Goleman's original premise was starting to play out.

An example of HOW would be to take the company or team through a few conversations to determine its core values. Most medium-to-large companies have likely devoted time to define a set of values unique to who they aspire to be, who their customers require them to be and what they believe will set them apart from competitors.

Empathy is often on that list of values, along with integrity, honesty, mutual respect and accountability — to name a few.

Essentially, an organisation's values are a huge part of its brand and identity. The belief here is that people will want to work for you, not just because you deliver a popular product or service, but because the culture in which they work helps them to thrive. They are more engaged and committed. In turn, so are your customers. You want customers to feel your values as a part of your brand. With the right values in place, you can build stronger performance. Two companies may deliver the same WHAT, but it's the HOW that differentiates between one having higher staff engagement and customer loyalty, while the other struggles to perform.

Many Kiwi and global companies now measure staff engagement annually, as they correlate high engagement with strong performance and results. The rapidly compressed cycles of change, up three-fold over the past decade, have also lifted the importance of staff engagement. With change now as a steady and relentless constant, it's important to be more connected with your team to ensure they have the right mindset associated with change. Based on life experience, many people view change as disruptive, a bad thing, sometimes outright scary. It is not uncommon for everyone in a group to have at least one personal story about a change initiative gone bad, where they were personally impacted in a negative way. This goes to the heart of trust. Once broken, it is difficult to regain. In today's business world, you can no longer afford to leave trust to chance.

Pandemic Revelations. With the increased cycles of change, there is also more vulnerability and uncertainty in the workplace — all part of living in an agile and interconnected world where we are encouraged to fail fast and morph quickly. With little notice, an internal or external event can wreak havoc on your best-laid plans. Consider the COVID-19 pandemic and its dramatic and immediate impact on our lives, and on livelihoods globally. As that scenario played out across nations, you could see the differences between strong and poor leadership and the impact both had on their public's confidence. Country leaders who minimised or distorted the pandemic were not seen as transparent and, consequently, they lost trust, respect and confidence. Watching America from afar was not a pretty picture. Having family and friends there made it even more painful. Politics definitely prevailed over humanity. Donald Trump's leadership during the COVID-19 response was nothing short of abhorrent. His dismissive 'hands off' approach and refusal to follow even the most basic safety guidelines from his own advisors most likely cost him a second term in office. Millions of Americans contracted the virus and, at time of print, the toll had moved beyond 500,000 lives lost because of his need to control the narrative, one that was self-absorbed, politically motivated, with no personal accountability for the outcome. In contrast, country leaders who led with transparency and honesty helped their citizens keep things in proper perspective, to stay positive and focused, and to feel empowered.

As a New Zealander, I was inspired by how our nation's leaders, united as one across our broad political spectrum, enabled Kiwis to believe with confidence that we could defeat an insidious and invisible enemy. We were an army of five million who became a global benchmark. Galvanised by strong leadership, we found our way together through this crisis. Even with resurges, there is a stronger resolve that comes with unity. As we well know, the 'call to arms' during periods of uncertainty in the broader realm of life is no different in the business world.

It pays for leaders to be more attuned to the constant emotional swirl happening around them, to understand the impact on their teams, and to help their people keep change and disruption in proper perspective. Even pre-COVID, disruption was no longer the exception. Navigating a business through major change is a huge component of growing a team's resilience. However, even with that constant swirl, you will not require a degree in psychotherapy to lead a team. You just need to understand the role you play in driving stronger connection and engagement. And to appreciate why these things are so important, especially as the pace of change builds.

The Four-Quadrant Model. What follows is a simple four-quadrant model that lays out the major components of EQ. This model represents the integration of constructs and ideas among scholars and practitioners spanning five decades of research and anecdotal reflection. If you have the time and interest, check out the wide array of information on EQ in an online search, or refer to the references listed in the book. If you prefer the highlights in a succinct and concise model, the one below will likely resonate with you.

EMOTIONAL INTELLIGENCE (EQ)

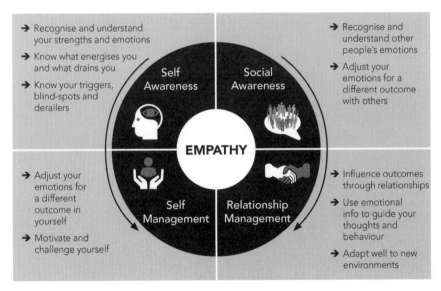

THE EQ MODEL: A REAL-TIME EXAMPLE
Self-Awareness

Rod is in a meeting with three members of his team. They run quality control for a small but quickly emerging IT firm, now in its fifth year with a steady growth trajectory. However, customer complaints are up over the last two quarters and there is now the real risk of having some critical projects stall — not a good thing for a growing business. As one of four members on the leadership team, Rod has felt tremendous pressure and has lost sleep worrying about the numbers that point to his team as having dropped the ball. After all, they are a critical link in driving customer retention and loyalty. He feels exposed under a spotlight that feels pretty intense at the moment.

Now, 15 minutes into the team meeting, Rod senses a major disconnect with Rajesh, Lynne and Matt. They seem to believe that skimping around the edges to save a dollar is more important than the company's value to always put the customer first. Tired and frustrated, no longer even listening to what they have to say, Rod wonders how this disconnect could have happened. His patience is growing thin and he is inclined to just tell them to stop whining and get with the programme. But he knows that won't be helpful. Rod knows from experience that his grumpy side does not serve him well when it comes to discussions like this. He is particularly mindful of a rough conversation he had just last week with Matt, so he knows that he must get his head into a better space now, or else things could go south real fast.

Self-Management

Rod is a big guy — both in height and girth. Given his size, he has learned that it is better for him to sit, especially when he is frustrated, to ground himself and be less intrusive into another person's space. As the team leader and a member of the leadership team, he has also learned that his rank, in and of itself, can be intimidating to people who report to him, even more so if he is frustrated or angry. Rod quickly plugs back into the conversation with his team, aware that his own internal dialogue has broken connection. Raj has been talking for the last two minutes, but it is clear that Matt and Lynne have started to shut down. He can tell it from their body language. Rod knows that he has to change the energy in the discussion quickly. But first, he has to get his head into the right space.

Rod now realises that he should have started the discussion on a more positive note. His own sense of urgency, coupled with mounting frustration, prompted him to dive right into the problem, which put the team on a defensive footing from the start. This is a very important conversation, so he needs to step back, lift up and do a reframe on what he wants to convey through his words, in his tone and his overall demeanour. Rod wishes he could do a re-take on the start of the meeting, but real life doesn't work that way. So, now he has to dial himself back into what Raj is saying. And also find a way to bring Matt and Lynne back into the conversation. This is easier said than done. He unfolds his arms and leans back a bit more in his chair, trying to put himself and his team at ease. This meeting has to end well.

Social Awareness

Rod realises that Raj, the most senior member of the team, is speaking on behalf of his two peers, so he opens up his energy even more by leaning into the conversation, listening now with intent. By doing so, he can feel the reconnect with Raj, who 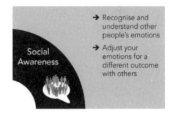 seems to breathe easier. Raj joined the company in its first year and is considered a steady guy. Rod really values Raj as his 2IC, but he has felt a bit detached from him over the past month. Now in the moment, it becomes clear that this conversation is long overdue. Yet, Rod knows that he has to navigate through it carefully. This is the toughest challenge he has faced as a team leader in a long while. He knows that he has to get everyone re-engaged quickly.

Rod senses that Matt is still a bit bruised from the tough performance review last week, so he wants an opportunity in this meeting to affirm him. He really likes Matt and wants him to do well, but also knows that Matt has to raise the bar on his performance based on feedback from other departments. And Lynne is only six weeks into the company, still finding her way and not yet inclined to put herself out there in any way. Rod hired Lynne because his gut told him that she would bring a step change to the lift they required as a team. He has been disappointed in how little Lynne has contributed, but now wonders if there is a correlation between his tension and her silence. Has the pressure from the CEO started to push down into the psyche of his team? Rod now realises that he is part of the problem here. This isn't a blame game. He has to own this with his team.

Relationship Management

→ Influence outcomes through relationships

→ Use emotional info to guide your thoughts and behaviour

→ Adapt well to new environments

Rod changes gears, almost 180 degrees after realising that, from the start of this conversation, the energy with his team has been negative. He stepped into the conversation in a frustrated mood, focusing on their mistakes and insinuating that their motives ran counter to the company's value on customer service. The CEO had given Rod a good bashing about the numbers just yesterday and, still frustrated, he is undoubtedly projecting that same negative energy onto them now. This is called 'displacement', when you unleash your own frustrations onto another person or group. To preserve your own self-image, it is easier to blame others than to accept that you are part of the problem. Rod realises that he has to own the problem with his team, starting with the fact that he has spent very little time with them over the past month. He has been managing them intensely, but not coaching them, and certainly not leading them. When people are over-managed, they feel controlled. When you coach people, they feel supported. Rod's pressures at the next level up have absorbed him. Through no fault of their own, his team has been directionless.

Rod decides to shift things into their proper perspective. He tells his team about some of the budgetary demands on him, as well as the company, over the past two quarters. Because he has owned the problem all by himself rather than bringing them into his thinking earlier, they would have very little context around their recent experiences with him, which have been mostly negative. Rod's intent was to get on top of the budget overruns quickly while sparing them the details, knowing how overloaded they are. He has pressured them to cut costs, but he has offered very little coaching to them on how to sustain a critical focus on quality. Raj, Matt and Lynne have been finding their way together, feeling unsupported and very loosely aligned with their leader. Raj is brave enough to now put this huge 'undiscussable' on the table. Rod listens and knows that he has to reconnect with his team in a sustainable way. They are running low on energy and wondering whether he values them. This is a make-or-break moment for him.

More so than ever before, Rod appreciates why a leader should never take connection with a team for granted. Healthy relationships require a sustained effort. Time for him to rebuild his team. They are decent people who deserve better.

Empathy at the Core

The example of Rod highlights that, to have high EQ, you are not required to always have things in perfect order. Good leaders are also humans who succumb to the pressures and stress of everyday life. The key to stronger EQ is being able to see the impact of your role in any problem or solution, more so sooner than later. It also entails the ability to flex in the moment, which means backing yourself sooner to go with your gut instinct when something does not feel right.

In the example with Rod and his team, you can see how empathy intersects and connects the four quadrants. Empathy sits at the very core of emotional intelligence. It entails both the ability to look inward and to project outward. It enables a connection with self, as well as with others. At its core sits compassion, which is what Rod's team was craving. As Brené Brown so eloquently points out in her TED Talk, 'The Power of Vulnerability', to show compassion for others requires you to first be compassionate with yourself. Rod had been hard on himself over the past month, which broke connection with his team. When empathy is in full throttle, the connection is palpable in both directions.

Time to explore the very core of EQ more deeply, to unpack the essence of empathy and what human connection is all about.

3

EMPATHY: WHAT IS IT?

The Power of Pathos. Twenty-four centuries ago, Aristotle advocated that empathy can be a powerful arrow in your leadership bow. To be accurate, he didn't use the word *empathy* in making his case. Instead, he used the word *pathos*. But the essence of both words is the same. Along with *logos* (logic) and *ethos* (character), Aristotle believed that pathos was an effective way to connect with other people, the premise being that humans are emotional creatures who have an inherent capacity to feel empathy. So, he coached leaders on how to persuade an audience by appealing to the emotions that already reside in them naturally. In today's language, you have to make an *emotional connection* with the team if you want them to hear your ideas and follow your lead with more passion.

Pathos was initially a communication technique used most often in rhetoric where the goal was to persuade a group of people to take a different point of view — often by invoking the thought of pain, suffering or loss. We have all had personal experiences where, on occasion, pulling the emotive cord works when you are striving to get something across the line. For example, people instinctively 'feel' for you when you genuinely put yourself out there, where you are truly exposed as imperfect, yet willing to give it a shot anyway. As humans, we instinctively relate to what that must feel like — and we usually feel for the person. This is pathos at its best, where you are able to genuinely influence people through your vulnerability. People really do connect with you better when you wear imperfection as a virtue, rather than as a vice. Aristotle coached leaders to work pathos a bit more to their advantage, especially those who weren't naturally good in this space.

Getting Under Empathy. Fast forward 24 centuries and there are dozens of books, numerous TED Talks and literally hundreds of articles about empathy online, most of them non-empirical. There are a lot of people writing and talking about empathy compared to even a decade ago. It is a topic gaining momentum in mainstream social media, most notably seen as central to the growing dialogue about why emotional intelligence is important in our lives. One thing seems to be a given across most of the dialogue: all roads to EQ seem to run through empathy. It is core to human connection.

The definitions do vary slightly across authors, as well as the broad spectrum of topics related to empathy — ranging from autism to xenophobia. There is a general belief that we are born with the capacity to experience empathy, although there are higher filters associated with acting on those feelings. Even with the multitude of opinions and perspectives out there, most of the definitions seem to circle around a few core themes that capture what this powerful word really means.

Even Scrooge has a Heart. First off, there seems to be universal agreement that the essence of empathy is most definitely about connection through caring, not just in humans but in all mammals. As the world of neuroscience has availed more knowledge on the limbic (emotive) brain, as well as the whole brain, there is strong consensus that biology underpins empathy. The basic capacity to recognise and respond to emotions is almost unmistakably innate; it can be achieved unconsciously and is apparent in infants as young as three weeks old.

Yes, certainly there are aspects of rational cognition that enable you to understand what it must be like for one of your peers on the team to prepare herself emotionally for a double mastectomy. If you are a guy, it perhaps even raises your own awareness about the prevalence of breast cancer in men. You have the capacity to understand things cognitively, even if you have never experienced something first-hand. Some people 'get it' by imagining what it must be like to live through a particular situation. As humans, we have the innate ability to imagine.

But it sometimes runs a bit deeper than a picture in your head of what something might be like, especially if you know the person, or are really close with someone who has experienced the same challenge. Even if you don't, you are still able to relate to the distress. You can connect with the fear that comes along with not being in control. You can imagine the dread of having a million dollar plan unravel right before your very eyes. You can relate to the angst of not knowing if your manager still backs you. You can imagine what it would feel like for your world to cave in, right in front of you, right now.

Have you ever sat across from another person whose world is at that very point? As their peer and even as their manager, it is very difficult not to feel their pain, particularly if you already have a connection through some kind of kinship. Feeling another person's pain goes beyond just being able to envision a picture in your head. It's more like a movie and you are simultaneously on the screen and in the audience. It is not uncommon to feel another person's pain viscerally. It's a human thing that enables us all to relate to certain experiences in life, no matter what our backgrounds.

When it comes to empathy, logic is best described as a complementary overlay that sits on top of a more fundamental energy rooted in the emotive brain — where you actually 'feel' the connection with another person through your ability to imagine. There's more about the hard-wiring that underpins empathy in Chapter 5.

A Proverbial Truth. The second theme related to empathy also stands out as a universal truth, probably best described as a proverb:

You should walk a mile in someone else's shoes before you dismiss them too quickly. To convey empathy implies that you have to truly understand what the experience is like for the person, perhaps even feel it, even if you have never been there yourself. As a manager, can you relate to what it must be like for one of your team members to be on the brink of burnout? Have you ever *really* walked around the shop floor to see things eye-level with what your team experiences every day? Or does your world begin and end at your office door?

Prior to the COVID-19 pandemic, workplace flexibility had started to gain more momentum, cited in some studies as the most important factor in whether a job candidate accepts a role, or whether someone decides to leave a company. Just 10 years earlier, workplace flexibility was considered a privilege, largely associated

> *Feeling another person's pain goes beyond just being able to envision a picture in your head. It's more like a movie and you are simultaneously on the screen and in the audience.*

with women who needed to balance the demands of family life and being part of a team at work. Increasingly, over the past decade, this privilege has become more of a perceived right, fortified by younger men who are now demanding the same flexibility to manage the blurred lines between work and home.

The COVID-19 pandemic forced all non-essential businesses to work virtually and far more flexibly than ever before. Even though many companies had such policies in place before the crisis, employees who requested flexibility often felt they were pushing against the grain, largely because many of the senior executives grew up in an era where 'being at work' meant that you were all together in a designated physical location. Before the pandemic, there was a prevalent mindset among senior executives that conveyed a subliminal message to their teams: 'If you are working from home, you must be goofing off.' Some people really struggled to ask for flexible arrangements because their managers never worked from home. It just goes to show the sheer power of behaviour over words. Even though the policies were in place, the behaviour of the senior leaders drove the true culture.

Throughout the pandemic, there has been greater empathy from CEOs and senior executives who had to walk in the shoes of their team members who occasionally work from home. At a more visceral level, business leaders now understand the demands of having to routinely juggle multiple priorities — often associated with parenting young kids, being accessible to teenagers, caring for elderly or disabled loved ones, studying for certifications, or simply making space in their lives to breathe a bit easier. Many leaders who had not previously worked from home quickly learned that you can, in most cases, work productively from a home office. In fact, many people were more productive in lockdown than they normally are in an open space work setting. The project management software company Atlassian reckons that, on average, you are likely to be interrupted 56 times each day in open space. It takes a couple of minutes to refocus after each interruption, amounting to around two hours of non-productive time in a typical workday. For many CEOs, the empathy gene kicked in big time when they had no choice but to live the experience of those people who really aren't goofing off at home, but instead are beavering away and getting loads of work done.

As we worked through COVID-19, you likely had far more time with those people in your life who really matter the most, but often take a back seat to your work when you come home from the office after a long day — especially for people who work 12-hour days. Prior to locking down into a virtual reality, many people struggled to find a balance that would enable them to be more present at home with their partners and kids. The pandemic actually sparked greater empathy across households. For the first time ever for many kids, they were able to see their parents 'at work', to hear the types of conversations they have, how much time they spend in meetings, even some of their frustrations that might otherwise be secluded in the workplace. Kids would have a better appreciation for why mum or dad needs a little space or downtime to chill out for an hour when they come home.

Partners in relationships also had to coordinate around a new normal, which entailed working a full-on day from home, watching and schooling the kids, taking care of pets, cooking and cleaning, all while tiptoeing gently around each other's psychological energy.

Partners who work outside the home now have greater empathy for the partner who manages those daily routines that keep their homelife intact. And, hopefully, parents have greater empathy for their kids, who had to make meaning of a scenario that is mind-boggling for even the most renowned scientists, let alone a four year old who knows something is not right, but cannot find the words to express herself.

The upsides of cutting out the commute time and the costs associated with face-to-face meetings, coupled with the heightened intimacy between peers and family accommodated by virtual technology, has already become a part of our new normal. Most of us have now experienced what advocates for workplace flexibility have known for years. Until you actually put those shoes on, it was difficult to understand their perspective. Now that most of us have walked that mile, it makes it so much easier to care. A clear upside to the pandemic has been stronger empathy for those people who require more day-to-day flexibility in their lives.

Human and Social Nuances. The third theme related to empathy takes us back to the first, which is that the basic capacity to recognise and respond to emotions is largely innate. Experiences that we associate with human connection, such as love, trust, compassion and hurt, have been empirically validated in an avalanche of studies in neurology that validate EQ as a real thing largely rooted in the limbic brain. It is indeed 'human' to feel for another person or group in pain. And, yet, it is clear human beings clearly make choices about whether to act on those same feelings.

Your biology definitely predisposes you to be moved by the plight of the person sitting next to you on the train. But the world around you and, to a large extent, the tribe you most identify with, has a major impact on how and whether you show empathy in a way that is meaningful to another person. Humans tend to ponder empathy far more than other mammals who succumb to raw innate instinct to help a kindred spirit in distress. I saw this first-hand at an elephant village in Sri Lanka. A baby elephant somehow got its foot caught in a chain in a pond, which caused it to scream loudly. Suddenly and with zero deliberation, the whole herd turned and rushed back with great speed and urgency to get the young one unstuck. Every single one of them turned on a dime, on instinct, to help one of their own in distress. As humans, we often ponder that same scenario as a choice.

As Goleman proposes, it would appear empathy is malleable and that humans play a major role with each other in how, or even whether, it gets expressed. Each of us has a certain comfort level expressing empathy, shaped largely by experiences across our lifetime. Some people can express empathy better than others, while others are more adept on the receiving end. What you do with this natural predisposition to 'feel' is heavily influenced by your life experiences, particularly with your family and the cultures you have grown up in.

Early in life, girls are more expressive with empathy than boys, which tracks along the same delineation into adulthood. The same gender distinction is replicated across mammal colonies. Some nationalities are more expressive with empathy than others. For example, roughly 30 per cent of the citizens in the Philippines choose nursing or health-related services as a profession, reflective of a cultural norm that values empathy and care for the elderly and disabled. In fact, the country is the largest exporter of nurses in the world. Conversely, other countries gain a reputation for being less empathetic, such as business leaders raised in the Netherlands who often relish being described as 'Dutch', which can be code or an excuse for 'He's going to be brutal with his feelings', as if to imply that being Dutch defies empathy. These are generalisations, of course, with many exceptions, but they reinforce how malleable empathy really is. Some cultures are warm while others are much colder. As horrid as it sounds, homosexuality is still a criminal offense in 73 countries around the globe, punishable by death in 10 nations, primarily clustered in Africa and the Middle East.

I am often asked how I rate New Zealand as an empathetic nation. I have heard some very heart-wrenching sentiments from immigrants who have not felt very welcome in New Zealand, particularly people who are black, brown or of Asian descent. Some people believe that xenophobia is alive and well here. An Islamic female immigrant contacted me a few years back to ask my advice on how she should react to her company asking her to remove her burqa, which they said was making some of their clients uncomfortable. She was torn between the need to hold true to who she is, but also to fit in and be accepted by the team. I really felt for her in that experience, especially knowing how far I had gone earlier in my life to fit in and be a good corporate citizen, not wanting to disturb the peace. This woman's burqa was my sexual orientation. It was easy for me to empathise with her dilemma. I was disappointed to hear that her manager could make such a request in an era when inclusion means that we can be genuine to who we truly are, which enables each person to bring more of their spirit to the table.

My personal experience migrating to New Zealand was much more positive, largely because I came over in an executive role with the nation's largest company, the perks of which meant that I didn't have to muddle through some of the minutiae or navigate around roadblocks and social hurdles that other people have clearly faced. Fonterra embraced me with incredible warmth, including board directors who invited me to their farms to learn more about the dairy sector and spend time with their families. In my first six months in New Zealand, I was on a farm nearly every weekend, sharing personal space and good times with some lovely people who wanted me to be successful.

Perspective is everything, I suppose. Living in America, I felt that my race and sexual orientation defined me. My experience in New Zealand has been very different. I now live in a country that, over the past decade, has legalised gay marriage, enacted legislation for sex workers to be safe from harm and induced

We are a nation clearly in stretch around inclusion, still finding our way through the maze of a more diverse profile.

major gun reform in the aftermath of the tragic Mosque shootings in Christchurch. Not to mention the incredible unity and kindness we showed for each other during the COVID-19 pandemic. We still have a long road ahead of us when it comes to genuine inclusion around the future demography of New Zealand. At my citizenship ceremony comprised of 997 people in 2008, roughly half of us were non-white, many with English as a second language. We are a nation clearly in stretch around inclusion, still finding our way through the maze of a more diverse profile. That said, I choose New Zealand over any other place on earth to spend the rest of my life. Many friends who are also immigrants share that sentiment.

Learned Compassion. This third theme around human and societal nuances to empathy then raises an important question. If you accept that empathy is the core of emotional intelligence, can you lift your own ability to be more empathetic in a way that really makes a difference? This is a common question. Can you really raise a person's EQ? The resounding consensus out there is 'yes, you most certainly can lift EQ'. From my own work with leaders, I believe that you can develop compassion. Absolutely. But it takes work and definitely is not easy. Two things help. First, if you want to show greater empathy to others, you must be reasonably insightful. This means that you must have a realistic grasp on who you are, what drives you, what derails you, the impact you have on other people — essentially all those things that enable you to stay in your optimal zone. Insight grows through personal experience and reflection. People who are insightful spend considerable time in personal reflection.

Secondly, if you want to show greater empathy, you must be motivated to change old ways. Is your interest in empathy a passing fad or a tick-the-box HR exercise? Or are you seriously interested in connecting with people at a more meaningful level? Your motivation will say a lot about your tenacity to push through old habits in order to learn and practise new behaviours. If your manager suggests that you work with a coach to minimise the 'noise' around your leadership, your motive could very well be to reduce the spotlight on yourself. This is an example of extrinsic motivation, which means that your goal is to satisfy the request of your manager, hence a sense of being obliged to follow through. Intrinsic motivation is more powerful because the desire to change comes from

> When it comes to empathy, the adage, 'Fake it till you make it' will not work. Caring is something that you cannot fake.

within, not because someone else requires you to follow through. This is the case with any serious effort to change behaviour or old habits that are working against you. To be successful, you need a greater sense of personal accountability and ownership.

Bottom line: you can most definitely build muscle around your empathy gene, particularly if you are able to grow insight and are personally motivated to try new ways of 'being' with other people. Unlike IQ, which is fairly stable, EQ gives you some room to play. Because you are focused on the essence of connection with empathy, you will see the immediate impact on interactions. But you have to really value caring. When it comes to empathy, the adage 'Fake it till you make it' will not work. Caring is something you cannot fake. As you have likely deduced, the personal goal to lead with greater empathy will most definitely take you closer to your own personal values.

What's Your Motive? There is debate among online contributors, authors and researchers about whether empathy is rooted in altruism or egotism. Altruism suggests your empathy is motivated solely by the need of the other person who may be hurting, whereas egotism suggests that your support is motivated by personal gain, even if just a quiet sense of self-appreciation. In the first instance, the person on the receiving end usually appreciates your support. It literally touches them in a way that is often hard for them to put into words. There is hopefully only the rare occasion when the person may ponder whether there is an ulterior motive behind your support. Most people are touched by genuine empathy and rarely ponder your motive unless you give them reason to.

Perhaps the true test of where you fall on the altruism–egotism spectrum is whether you can give to others anonymously. As you explore getting your head around empathy a bit more, maybe this topic of 'root cause' goes to the heart of what motivates you as a person. Wherever you land on the spectrum, it's rarely a show-stopper when it comes to the outcome. Compassion is in the eye of the receiver, not the giver. If you are genuine and care, people will know it. If you are acting out of self-interest, people will also know it. The gift is secondary to what they feel coming from you.

Breaking it All Down. When we pull all of the brainpower, wisdom and perspective together on the topic of empathy, we land on a definition that pretty much captures what we already know intuitively. Empathy wears a halo, not horns. It is a feeling that you can tap into in another person, like when they suddenly stop and really listen to what you are telling them. It is also something that other people can tap into in you, like when your heart is captivated by a story you overhear from two strangers in the seats behind you on the train.

Empathy can be conveyed with purpose, or it can touch you randomly. It will often catch you off guard, as experienced by many guys who tear up in movie theatres under the protection of darkness. Empathy can make you happy or it can frustrate you. It can make someone's day, even their year, especially when their energy is depleted. To truly feel empathy, it may require you to spend a bit more time consciously walking around in your own shoes. Are you compassionate enough with yourself? Empathy is all these things and then some.

Our working definition below pulls it all together:

EM-PA-THY
[ˈɛmpəθi]

NOUN
1. A blended set of natural and learned skills core to the construct of EQ.
2. The need to care about and connect with other people emotionally.
3. The ability to understand, even to viscerally feel for, another person, without judgement; the experience of walking in another person's shoes.
4. Support that comes from a genuine place of understanding, care and a desire to help.
5. A meaningful connection, within and beyond yourself.

4

TWO SIDES OF THE SAME COIN

Sympathy and Empathy. These two words sometimes get used interchangeably, although they have different meanings. They both have the link to pathos, for sure. So, how are they different? Let's start with sympathy — a word we often use when someone loses a loved one. A loss of any type typically will evoke sympathy in others. We tend to associate sympathy with expressions of support and sorrow, especially when someone is grieving. The dozens of spontaneous memorials across New Zealand, adorned with flowers and gifts, to show support and love for the Muslim community in the aftermath of the tragic Mosque shootings in Christchurch is a perfect example of what sympathy looks like.

When you sympathise with someone, you express support, comfort, even pity for what they are going through — without necessarily understanding, or possibly never having experienced their plight. The classic sympathy card captures the essence of the term. You feel sorry for someone who may be in distress. The words in the card, which you choose carefully and sometimes write yourself, are intended to nullify pain. You are focused on the person's distress and your goal is to support, comfort or even show pity. You may not be able to personally relate to why your mate at work is so distraught over losing a pet dog, but you know that he is hurting, so you take a few extra minutes out of your day to call and show support. Maybe you even send a thoughtful card to brighten his day. At its most basic level, when you sympathise with someone, your primary aim is to help alleviate their distress or discomfort. You want them to feel better.

Empathy goes a bit deeper and is more connecting. When you empathise with someone, you go beyond expressions of support or comfort. To donate to a homeless shelter once a year might be considered a way to sympathise with those people who live on the streets — without fully understanding or being able to feel what that experience must actually be like for them. To put yourself in their shoes at a visceral level, would you be willing to sleep (for even one night) in a cardboard box enclosure, or on a park bench, in cold and wet weather? Cities in New Zealand and Australia have sponsored a yearly event where corporate donors can spend a night out on the street, side by side with homeless citizens, to experience the raw sense of exposure that comes with not having secure shelter around you.

To be clear, empathy doesn't require you to become the other person. You can feel for someone without losing objectivity on that being their experience, not yours. Healthy empathy is grounded in your ability to maintain a clear 'self–other' distinction. If the line blurs and that distinction is not present, this can result in *emotion contagion*, which then nullifies your ability to support the other person. In psychology, this is called *countertransference*. Empathy requires you to understand, and sometimes feel, what it is like to walk in that person's shoes, while acknowledging that your conclusions or decisions may still differ. In the first instance, it is about being understood, which many people describe as a feeling.

The African-American poet, Maya Angelou, is renowned for her compelling quote: 'I've learned that people will forget what you said, people will forget what you did, but people will never forget how you made them feel.' That quote captures empathy in a nutshell. People can *feel* the difference between being understood and being judged. When you judge another person, they fold their arms like a shield over their chest, to ward off the attack. When you understand another person, they unfold their arms and open their energy to you. Your body posture is usually a dead giveaway as to whether you feel a genuine connection with another person.

A Beautiful Synthesis. Then there are models that position sympathy and empathy together as complementary elements under the same construct, where sympathy is sometimes referred to as *empathic concern* or, more commonly, *compassion*. For humans and other mammals, compassion is often shown through outward expressions of support, such as a cuddle or hug, taking a protective stance, giving of time, effort, even money. The overlay model is appealing because it doesn't delineate sympathy and empathy as distinctive — because they truly aren't. There is caring in both.

When you delineate between the two as distinct entities, sympathy often sounds more superficial, less deep and less caring. The overlay model helps to bring the two together in a synthesis, with sympathy actually being the deepest level of empathy, manifested through prosocial and helping behaviours. People are so moved by what they have experienced to the point where they are motivated beyond just 'feeling the pain'. In this context, donating to a homeless shelter is viewed as the deepest level of empathy, rather than a superficial 'tick the box' gesture to wash away guilt for not making time to give more of yourself.

'Two sides of the same coin' is probably the best way to capture the best of sympathy and empathy. The coin is called *caring*. Sympathy is about feeling for someone. Empathy is about feeling with someone. You can clearly empathise with someone while also expressing your sympathy through actions aimed at alleviating distress, discomfort or pain. You may also be motivated to give because of an emotional connection that is not yet rooted in a deep knowledge of the other person. *You can't explain it, but you feel like you need to do something for this person.*

I remember the young, white civil rights advocates in the 1960s who came out to join black marchers as they walked anxiously down streets lined with white supremacists in the southern states of America. Black Americans were protesting against the presumption that we should accept our status as second-class citizens. By joining the black marchers in the street, the white supporters got a first-hand experience of what it is like to be spat on, called hateful names and punched. Yes, empathy is about understanding what the other person is going through. The insight is deep. But it shouldn't be regarded as a more sophisticated sympathy. The two are interconnected and move around each other fluidly.

In the case of those white marchers, sympathy preceded empathy. The gesture of saying 'we will march with you' is a great example of sympathy — an expression of support. It wasn't until those white marchers were eye-to-eye with anger and venom coming at them from all directions that they could, for the first time, fully appreciate what it *feels like* to be hated simply for being who they are. Prior to the protests, they could have imagined what it must be like. That is cognitive empathy. But it is a completely different experience to actually feel it, especially for the first time. That is when empathy would have kicked in for them at a very palpable level.

Fast forward five decades to protests all over the world in response to the murder of George Floyd, the African-American man who died at the hands of police, sparking deep conversations about whether racism, in and beyond America, is yet another pandemic the world has to combat. Reflecting back on the racial protests in 1968, the great majority of marchers on the streets were black. The protests associated with Floyd's death, symbolic of thousands of stories like his, brought people of all races out to march together in a unified stance against police brutality and racism. This time around, the scale of empathy had magnified significantly, a colourful tapestry of people

It wasn't until those white marchers were eye-to-eye with anger and venom coming at them from all directions, that they could, for the first time, fully appreciate what it feels like to be hated simply for being who they are.

from all racial and ethnic backgrounds holding signs, shouting 'Black Lives Matter' and, in some cases, tear gassed and arrested for taking a stand. That was a real-time distinction between what it means to feel 'with' someone rather than 'for' them. The connection is definitely deeper.

Make a Difference. Whether we are talking sympathy or empathy, the goal is to show that you do care about the impact of 'every day' life on the people around you, at work and at home. And also, for those people who live beyond your borders who you feel connected with, for whatever reason.

Feel good about making a donation of money or time to your favourite charity or social cause. You simply may not have the personal space or funds to travel to Costa Rica or Sudan to make a difference where it matters most on the ground. But your sympathy is a way to show that you care. And that support will have a big impact, even if you are still yet to stand at their ground zero. Empathy grows with time on some things. Don't wait to express care until you fully understand why you do. If something grabs your heart, it means you care. In most cases, sooner is probably better than later to make a real difference.

Where can you make a difference in someone's life today? Before the week is out? Perhaps even with the test of anonymity? No need to self-flagellate with an altruism whip if you lean toward egotism. Sometimes it really does matter to the recipient to know who you are. I think it is fine if you want people to see what you value and endorse publicly, to have your name sit beside something as a tangible sign of your support. If your heart is in the right place, don't overthink it.

One coin, two sides: huge impact.

5

WE'RE WIRED FOR IT

Cuddles and Hugs. Empathy seems to have deep roots in our brains and bodies, and in our evolutionary history. Elementary forms of empathy have been observed in our primate relatives, and studied most extensively in gorillas, chimpanzees and even rats. Pet owners across the globe have experienced the occasional warm nudge or cuddle from a dog or cat who senses that their 'pack leader' is distressed or sad. Infants as young as three weeks exhibit the same qualities of caring with their primary caretakers. There is no wonder why our emotive brain is also called the mammalian brain. Mammals really do enjoy warmth from each other.

The ability to show empathy has been associated with two different pathways in the brain, and scientists are convinced that some aspects of empathy can be traced to mirror neurons. These are cells in the brain that fire when we observe someone else perform an action in much the same way that those cells would fire if we performed that action ourselves. Empathising with another person's feelings relies on the activation of these neural networks to support the first-person experience of those feelings.

The next time you are at a comedy club watching a person at the mic struggle to connect with the audience, your biology is the likely trigger that causes you to chuckle in support, even if the jokes aren't funny. Your mirror neurons enable you to imagine yourself in the same situation, standing up there and looking into a sea of unimpressed eyes. Even if you don't know the person, your first thought is, 'Damn, that must be tough.' Your mirror neurons enable you to replicate the theatre in your mind's eye, this time with you at the mic. The good news to take away from this is that even your worst critics can't help but feel for you in situations where you may be on the spot and struggling a bit. The empathy they feel for you just may translate into one of them stepping up to help you out. This is an example of how vulnerability, when worn well, can spark connection.

The Power of Story. One very tangible indicator that leaders understand employee engagement better is the uptick in their focus on storytelling as a leadership tool. The vapours from the old management paradigm, which were still apparent in the early 2000s, reminds us just how much we overplayed logic in those days. The emphasis was on a rational connection between partners, that is, that makes good business sense. The thinking was that if you made a strong logical argument for why we should go in a certain direction, this would be good enough to get people over the line. Put up a PowerPoint slide with lots of numbers, charts and graphs — and appeal to people through their neo-cortex, the rational brain.

Things are different now. Again, the advent of EQ has helped. Since then, businesses have been paying more attention to the emotive brain, which is where the more sustainable connection happens for humans. Back to the power of storytelling and the difference this technique has made in people getting engaged around a topic at a primal level. Here's what we know. When a person hears a story, there is this fascinating process called neural entrainment, which is best described as the brain unfolding a theatre and stage in front of you, there in your mind's eye, where you can place yourself there as an observer to the story being told. The words 'once upon a time' are a spark for neural entrainment to kick in. People simply can't help but plug into a good story.

We see it with kids all the time. They are absolutely captivated by stories, long before their rational brains kick into full gear. The sheer joy on the faces of kids who sit in wonder as the story unfolds says volumes about how powerful the emotional connection can be. So, why haven't we leveraged this powerful storytelling tool in business prior to now? It all comes back to the dominant mindset that was in place only two decades ago. As adults, our brains don't grow numb around a good story. It's just that, by the time we become adults, particularly in formal education and the business world, we have been taught to overplay reason and underplay emotion. Twenty years ago, someone who opened a presentation with a story would have been viewed as unique, eccentric and perhaps a bit out there. Today, we are disappointed when it doesn't happen.

The Hard Wiring. The domain of pain has been one very prominent area of study to help understand the impact of mirror neurons. In a typical experiment, participants who are wired to scan their physiological responses either receive painful stimulation to body parts themselves, or are presented with pictures or cues that indicate that another person is currently experiencing pain. By then comparing the brain activations that are elicited by the first-hand experience of pain with those purely elicited by the vicarious observation of another person in pain, researchers have repeatedly found evidence of shared neuronal networks.

We tend to share another person's pain with greater empathy if they are like us, on the same team. No wonder businesses have started to advocate the 'one team' mentality across the enterprise, as opposed to each function seeing itself as a separate team.

To get technical about what goes down in these networks, a portion of the anterior insula and a specific part of the anterior cingulate cortex are consistently activated, both during the experience of pain as well as when vicariously feeling the suffering of others. This is one reason why some people simply cannot watch movies, or graphic news reports, that show other people in pain. It can be equally painful for the observer, even if the actor is a qualified stunt person.

To be clear, it's not an 'all or none' thing with the mirror neurons and our ability to feel another person's pain. Studies do reveal that empathic brain responses can vary based on certain factors. There are person-specific characteristics, such as gender and age, and there are context-specific factors. An example of the latter is how the perceived integrity (or lack thereof) of the person in pain will determine how much empathy the observer feels. You can imagine this very factor makes it possible for witnesses to watch a person be executed, particularly if they believe the pain is warranted. This is a graphic and perhaps disturbing example, but it illustrates the point well.

Another context-specific factor is whether or not the perceived victim of pain is a member of the tribe. We tend to share another person's pain with greater empathy if they are like us, on the same team. No wonder businesses have started to advocate the 'one team' mentality across the enterprise, as opposed to each function seeing itself as a separate team. The emotive bond across the teams is stronger if they view the competition as the enemy, not each other.

Although empathy has been studied most extensively in the domain of pain, there have also been substantive studies on how other sensory experiences, such as touch, disgust, taste and social rewards, impact on our willingness and ability to 'feel with' another person. The hard wiring intricately spans the rational and emotive components of the brain, making it possible to imagine and feel at the same time, such as being held or caressed, even if in your own fantasies. The neural pathways enable you to enjoy the sensation of taste while watching a television commercial, or vicariously feel joy for someone receiving an award, or walk past a guy who is running away from others in hot pursuit and immediately decide to intervene, based only on the visuals around you. These sensations happen immediately and reinforce the importance of biology in whether the connection with someone is positive or negative within a flash of meeting them. Personal experiences in your life clearly play a role in the sensation, sometimes described as intuition. We often let the rational brain prevail over intuition rather than listening closely to what our physiology is telling us. Sometimes it is important to follow your gut.

The research and data supporting the hard-wiring of empathy are compelling. And it appears that the message has resonated broadly within the business world over the past decade. Unlike the incessant debate over whether global warming is real, neurologists have given business leaders ample rationale to pronounce broadly: *EQ is most definitely for real.* Empathy is hard-wired and the business world must now figure out the best ways to leverage emotional connection as a source of competitive advantage. That's how real and important it is for success in business, as well as in life.

6

THE BUSINESS CASE FOR EMPATHY

Trust the Stats. In 2021, the discussion of empathy in the workplace goes far beyond considering it a 'soft skill' or some type of passing management fad. Employers must work harder to attract and retain talented people on their teams, particularly with people under the age of 35 who will spend, on average, three years with a given company. Contrast that with just two generations ago, when loyalty was defined by a gold watch after 25 years of service. Young people today live in a different world where they expect more fulfilment from a work experience, including greater workplace flexibility. There is now a very strong correlation between empathetic work cultures and tangible business outcomes, most notably with employee retention and engagement. Companies know how important it is to hold on to talented people who deliver with commitment.

When you consider the consistent finding across global studies that verify how roughly 90 per cent of employees, across large and small businesses, say they are more likely to stay with an empathetic employer, it is no wonder that companies are placing stronger emphasis on developing leaders who wear emotional intelligence well. As part of any employer's value proposition, it is hard to ignore the facts. The correlation between engagement and positive business outcomes has never been stronger. As Goleman proposes, empathy plays a huge role.

In today's labour market, organisations really must differentiate themselves and manage their brands with greater purpose to attract new talent and retain their current high performers. Across the broad realm of research on staff engagement, employees continue to report that they are far more engaged with an empathetic employer — back to the earlier points around workplace flexibility as a relevant example. By driving improved productivity through talent retention, empathy is more important than ever to achieving critical business goals such as greater revenue and profits, coupled with lower turnover and recruitment costs.

Goleman incites us to expand the lens on those things that load on people and culture. To quote Peter Drucker, 'culture eats strategy for breakfast.' In today's business world, most progressive leaders realise how true that really is. But this has not always been the case in the business world. Pre-EQ, there was a much heavier focus on the hardware that had to be in place to ensure business stability. Managing a business was about infusing processes, systems, protocols, regulations — all those things that often require intense oversight and scrutiny, especially when the pressure is on. In that era, businesses were led by management teams, not leadership teams. Process and procedure prevailed over speed and agility. You didn't hear much talk about empowerment or engagement back then, which really is not that long ago when you realise the transition from managing to leading others only started to gain real traction at the turn of the twenty-first century.

It almost seems a luxury now to imagine leaving a business model untouched for years, certain that the underlying assumptions will hold firm.

In just a span of two decades, the prevalent mental model has shifted more fervently toward leading rather than managing businesses and people. We once valued the certainty of stability over the uncertainty of disruption. Disruption was once seen through a negative lens back when we had the luxury of being able to nail things down and leave them intact for the better part of a decade. Change and intentional disruption were truly exceptions under that lens, certainly not the norm. It almost seems a luxury now to imagine leaving a business model untouched for years, certain that the underlying assumptions will hold firm. In today's context, that seems irrational, particularly for businesses that have now embraced speed, agility and the ability to fail fast and move onto the next curve quickly. COVID-19 has certainly levelled the playing field on that front. If you cannot adapt quickly, you will not survive.

The Paradox of Change. So, how does empathy factor into this steady and upward shift in mindset — one that moves the psychological energy from that of managing people to a different level of engagement through coaching and leadership? From an anthropological vantage, it seems paradoxical to move to a prevalent mentality that values disruption, especially since human beings are wired to perceive sudden change as a threat. As a leader, you can spark anxiety and vulnerability in people when you ask them to break a current pattern, one they have come to associate with stability in their lives. People feel exposed when they are asked to step away from certainty to wander down a path that is not neatly paved, or worse yet, to navigate into a fog where they can't see two feet in front of them. Change is a scary proposition for many people. You can see why trust is so important in a person's willingness to let go and move forward. The paradox requires us to push through disruption as quickly as possible to get to a new curve, where we can then stabilise things again. In a world where COVID-19 scenarios are likely to resurface, we have learned that agility and adaptability are no longer optional skills to navigate through life.

Process helps to mitigate anxiety in the face of uncertainty, but it does very little to invigorate energy or ownership for the path you are now on.

49

This is where leadership makes all the difference. Process helps to mitigate anxiety in the face of uncertainty, but it does very little to invigorate energy or ownership for the path you are now on. Wearing your management hat, you are likely to tell people to trust the process and ask them to follow your lead. Wearing your leadership hat, you inspire a sense of purpose around the end goal and then ignite the best in your people to own the path forward. Yes, the change process is still required to get us from here to there, but it is not what actually galvanises the team. That energy comes from what you unleash in them, especially through your belief in them.

As a leader, you create the conditions for your team to be successful. You take the pressure off yourself to be the sole architect of their future. It should be a shared accountability around owning the vision for success. You ensure that they are working in a culture that enables them to thrive. Then you constantly remind your people that their voices and perspectives are required to drive the organisation's success. You give them the opportunity to be heard and valued in an inclusive culture, not because the process requires it, but because you genuinely believe there is real value in their views.

When you listen to your team because the change process requires you to, the end result is typically a fair degree of cynicism. When you listen to your team with the intent to learn, understand and incorporate the best ideas from them, the end result is a team with a strong sense of connection and ownership. When two or more people are truly connected, empathy is the energy that holds them together.

More Clout. The empirical support for building empathetic companies has continued to grow over the past half-decade. A 2018 study from *Harvard Business Review* found that empathetic companies outperform their callous counterparts by 20 per cent. The study also highlighted that when people feel understood themselves, they are more receptive to others' concerns — and team cohesion and collaboration follow suit. People are also more prone to take risks, believing that they will be supported, rather than punished, if they fail. An empathetic workplace equals an engaged workforce, and that consistently translates to business success.

The Consortium for Research on Emotional Intelligence in Organizations reported a correlation between empathy and increased sales, higher performing managers of product development teams and increased performance in highly diverse teams. Their research also showed that empathy improves leadership ability and facilitates effective communication.

A 2015 study by the Center for Creative Leadership corroborated how empathy is positively related to job performance. Managers who show more empathy toward direct reports are viewed as better performers in their job by their managers. The findings were consistent across the sample: empathic emotion as rated from the leader's subordinates positively predicts job performance ratings from the leader's boss.

An empathetic workplace equals an engaged workforce, and that consistently translates to business success.

Empathy also enables leaders to create environments of open communication and feedback, understand and navigate the problems employees face, validate what their employees are going through and anticipate the needs of the team. On a team where empathy is strong, people are more attuned to the people around them, the same sentiment that you feel in a family environment.

The Bottom Line. Twenty-four centuries after Aristotle advocated the importance of empathy, the empirical data strongly supports his thesis. An empathetic workplace equals an engaged workforce, which translates into tangible business success. Just two decades ago, you never heard anyone talk about employee engagement. The primary objective was to make sure that employees were 'satisfied'. By today's standards, that word seems like such a banal thing. When it comes to customers, business leaders landed on that same insight sooner. Satisfied customers were likely to return for another purchase. Delighted customers were likely to bring someone along with them.

The magic works the same with employees. Satisfied employees are likely to stay with you unless something more compelling comes along. Engaged employees not only stay longer, but they are your biggest ambassadors for attracting new talent and retaining customers. All told, this is a very compelling business case for why empathy matters.

With the world in a constant swirl, can you really afford to *not* invest in building an empathetic workplace? That question would have been worded differently a mere 20 years ago. The old paradigms have truly shifted. What about you?

7

THE RULE OF THREE

Head, Heart and Action. Things in threes tend to stick more in the human psyche. Many people call this the rule of three. Speech writers are across this rule and go out of their way to help leaders resonate more powerfully with an audience, especially if the goal is to get people fired up about something. In public speaking, the rule of three is when you use three statements to drive home a single and powerful message. 'Blood, sweat and tears' is all about a deeper sense of commitment, especially when pushing through adversity. 'Government of the people, by the people, for the people' was Abe Lincoln's unity cry for a divided nation. 'Life, liberty and the pursuit of happiness' are considered unalienable rights. 'He tangata, he tangata, he tangata' reinforces people first, above all else.

And then there is *head, heart and action.* You have undoubtedly heard this expression, if not used it yourself to make a particular point. Perhaps without realising it, your use of these three words speaks to the three vital dimensions that culminate in empathy. It is a catchy phrase, often depicted in a drawing that shows a human head, the heart and a pair of hands — connected together to reinforce the integration of all three. Integration implies integrity, which is the state of being whole and undivided. These three words together speak to a wonderful sense of wholeness. In sync, they define human connection.

Head. In the research on empathy, the official name for this dimension is cognitive empathy. You don't have to feel what a person is feeling in order to show empathy. Sometimes it is very important that a person feels understood for why they feel a certain way, not that they are expecting you to feel their pain or joy. That cognitive connection means that you are trying to follow their logic, their path to getting to a point where it makes sense for them to be angry or joyful. You don't have to believe in what they believe, but it is connecting for them to believe that you understand how they got there. You are then far less likely to say to them, 'Oh you shouldn't feel that way.' People don't feel empathy when you tell them how they should feel. They feel judged.

Heart. The official name for this dimension is emotional empathy. Sometimes your connection with the other person goes beyond just understanding why they feel a certain way. Sometimes you have been through a similar experience, such as losing a job or even a child, or something close enough to where you feel a more compelling connection. You may feel sad with them in a way that doesn't happen with cognitive empathy. In fact, depending on how well you navigated through your own personal pain, sometimes your heart will pull you in deeper than you imagined, where you break connection with the other person, who then grows worried about you. If you have ever had a friend say to you, 'This isn't about you, it's about me', you understand the point. To have optimal impact, you really have to keep your heart in check.

Action. This is called compassionate empathy. Compassion is a beautiful word because it conveys care, concern and warmth. A friend once told me that her manager came to the hospital where she was recuperating from major surgery, and gently snatched her laptop out of her hands, telling her that her health and speedy recuperation were far more important than any work deadline. She could tell that he was there to make a point. The round trip drive to and from the hospital had taken up two hours of his day, plus he stayed 30 minutes to meet and chat with her family before leaving. He agreed to leave the laptop with her, but he enlisted her two sons as 'wardens' to make sure the patient would not do any official work. My friend cried when her manager left the room, touched by his compassion. Action goes a notch beyond understanding and being able to feel another person's pain. It is about doing something that matters.

Three Profiles in Empathy. When it comes to empathy, the rule of three really is a compelling synergy. Over the next three chapters, *head, heart and action* will come alive through nine short case stories that will help to illuminate the profile around each of the three elements of empathy. The first eight stories are based on recurrent themes that have emerged in my work with leaders at all levels across several decades. Please note that the characters are prototypes, not based on any specific person's experience. The ninth and final case story is a real one from my own personal experience earlier in life. Across all the stories, you will likely empathise with and relate to a number of the characters as they explore ways to strengthen connection with others.

8

COGNITIVE EMPATHY: THREE CASE STORIES

DEFINITION
At a rational level, trying to understand how the other person feels and how that feeling is connected to their thinking, even if it runs counter to your own beliefs.
Making a concerted effort to understand, without judgement, what another person is thinking and why.
Often referred to as perspective-taking.

WHAT IT ENTAILS
- Thought
- Understanding
- Collaboration
- Intellect

BENEFITS
- Helps in negotiations
- Motivating other people
- Understanding diverse viewpoints
- Ideal for virtual meetings

PITFALLS
- Can be disconnected from or ignore deeply felt emotions
- Does not put you in another person's shoes in a felt sense

Case Story 1: What's in a Name?

This is the story of Emirhan Ozdemir. He is from Turkey, born and raised in Ankara, the second largest city and the nation's capital. Emirhan left Turkey following university when he was 25, to pursue deeper experience in his technical field. He was also in hot

pursuit of a romance, which everyone predicted wouldn't last, and they were right. Emirhan initially lived in London for three years and then decided to migrate to New Zealand after researching a role with a utilities company in the energy sector. He caught their interest after some back and forth on LinkedIn, then in several focused discussions with a recruiter who liked his expertise and attitude.

Emirhan joined the team in Wellington 10 weeks earlier. He introduced himself by his given name in the interview, which didn't seem to be a problem then, but on the first day on-site with the team, he found that several people struggled to pronounce his name. This was not a new thing for Emirhan, especially when travelling through the western world, and especially since arriving in New Zealand. His natural response was to lessen the pressure on people who looked uncomfortable when trying to absorb his name. He had been very patient with people who asked him to repeat his name several times in order to get it right. He didn't mind that at all, especially with people who seemed to know the difference it made for him to hear his name pronounced correctly.

One week after joining the team, Emirhan's manager started to call him 'M'. He told Emirhan that it would make it easier for the team if they could shorten his given name, to take the pressure off anyone who might be afraid to offend him. His manager said that calling him 'M' will help to nullify the awkwardness others were feeling. The request to change his name did not feel very consultative to Emirhan. It felt more like 'your name is now M'.

Emirhan didn't think much about it at first. He liked the idea that he could make it easier on his peers to help reduce their discomfort over not being able to pronounce his name. Like many people who are new to a company or team, he wanted to fit in and be accepted — with minimal noise. He even told himself that being given a nickname is somewhat endearing. It is funny what the brain does to help alleviate pressure, the most profound defence mechanism being our ability to rationalise something that doesn't seem right. When people are trying hard to fit in and be accepted, they tend to rationalise something as okay, which otherwise would not fly.

A new colleague, Cheryl, joined the team after Emirhan's tenth week and upon meeting for the first time, she introduced herself and asked him his name. He said, 'They call me M'. Cheryl said, 'What's your given name?' He said, 'Emirhan.' She said, 'That's not difficult to pronounce at all. I would like to call you "Emirhan" if you don't mind.'

It wasn't until Cheryl called him by his proper name that Emirhan realised how much he had missed the connection to a huge part of his identity — his own given name. Hearing it from his new colleague felt so validating, almost nourishing; it was a difficult emotion for him to put into words. For the first time since his new name was assigned, he felt like a whole person, not marginalised by a simple letter in the alphabet. That was when it really dawned on him that he had made too big a sacrifice, conceding his identity to a single letter, to fit in with the team and be considered acceptable on their terms. This describes the classic tension between fitting in and standing out, where your goal is to strike a balance without compromising your authenticity.

Over the next couple of weeks during team meetings, Cheryl kept referring to Emirhan by his given name. But his manager and other peers continued to call him 'M'. There didn't seem to be any ill intent on their part. It was simply more convenient for them. Emirhan could not help but reflect on how odd it was that they all decided, without him being present, what his name would be. Even though he began to ponder the scenario deeply, he remained silent. It was not lost on him that his colleagues were not following Cheryl's example.

Then one day when 'M' wasn't at the meeting, Cheryl put the topic squarely on the table with the team, suggesting they consider what it would feel like to have a team decide that they were going to change your name, for their convenience, not to have to put themselves out to take a mere five seconds to learn how to pronounce it correctly.

With that challenge, Cheryl got their attention. She told them that it really was not that difficult to pronounce the three syllables that made up Emirhan's name. She called out that his name was no more difficult than saying 'Marilyn' or 'Sebastian', both of whom were on the team. She explained to them that many immigrants to New Zealand and other western nations, especially from Asian or Middle Eastern nations, often find themselves in a scenario where their name is shortened or changed altogether. Or, to avoid the awkwardness, they go ahead and change their name in advance, to make it easier for the majority group. Cheryl then made the point that a person's name validates them for who they are, not who we need them to be. She asked them to imagine going to live and work in a foreign country where their biggest priority would be to fit in and be accepted. By going the extra mile to pronounce a person's given name correctly, you show that you value them for who they are, not for making you feel less anxious.

For the first time since his new name was assigned, he felt like a whole person, not marginalised by a simple letter in the alphabet.

Cheryl opened her teammates eyes to something very important in the diversity and inclusion space. None of them had ever been in the awkward position of having to accept a new name to accommodate the team's comfort. But they got it when she pointed it out; it was an 'a-ha' moment for most of them, none of whom had stopped to put themselves in Emirhan's shoes. They had not intended to offend Emirhan, but they never considered what it would be like to be told that the team had given you a new name. Cheryl's words started to sink in. While none of them had been there before personally, they understood what that experience would be like for their colleague. Within the next day, 'M' was again Emirhan.

Emirhan now had a personal story to tell about inclusion. He vowed never to lose his identity again for the sake of fitting in and craving acceptance. Quite fitting for a man who wears a name that translates in Turkish as 'one who commands and reigns.'

Case Story 2: Can We Both Be Right?

This case story highlights the inherent tension that often exists between business units and corporate centres; HR being one of those central functions.

Pip Brown, the HR Director, was driving a huge culture initiative, which she described as transformational, to be measured (hopefully) by a significant lift in employee engagement and business results. In her first year, this was Pip's top priority. She had joined the company six months earlier to help design and lead this transformation. The CEO convinced her to come on board to help turn the negative tide on customer retention, which had become a real problem over the past two years.

The Sales Director, Chris Hagen, had been with the company for nearly 12 years. His team had some hard targets to hit that year and he really couldn't be bothered with this stuff that took up a lot of his team's time, for what he believed to be of minimal benefit. Historically, he had not been a champion of HR initiatives. He had never bought into all the hoopla around company values and mission statements and visioning sessions. For Chris, you ran a successful business if everyone understood their role and you let them be to deliver. His motto was, get rid of all the other stuff that inevitably distracted him and the sales team from nailing their monthly targets. Especially now, with the pressure of two consecutive bad years under his watch. They had to focus harder on delivery. Forget all this nonsense about finding our purpose. They had hard targets to hit.

Over the past six months, Pip and Chris had clashed swords at the leadership table — the classic inherent tension between centralised programmes versus autonomy in the field to get the real work done. Chris kept making the point that his team were smart people who did not have to go through days of culture training to understand how to sell beer and beverages to grocery chains, restaurant and pub owners. He said to Pip, 'they are hard-wired to do this in their sleep.' Pip rebutted with her own experience and a number of studies that proved the adage, 'culture eats strategy for breakfast' — her point being, you won't hold on to a talented sales force, and thereby key customers, unless you agree on core purpose and values. The two of them went back and forth with this debate, over and over again, like two kids bouncing feverishly on each side of a seesaw, one hoping to topple the other. It was apparent that neither was listening to the other.

The two of them went back and forth with this debate, over and over again, like two kids bouncing feverishly on each side of a seesaw, one hoping to topple the other. It was apparent that neither was listening to the other.

The CEO finally beckoned them both in together for a much-needed conversation, highlighting how the tension between them had started to impact on the leadership team dynamic, based on conversations he had had with their peers. Neither Pip nor Chris were surprised, as it only made sense people would infer they were at war, especially with the very tangible tension between the two of them. Using a military analogy, the CEO made the case that the troops will typically line up behind their respective generals to do battle with the enemy. In this case, the enemy was inside the company, not the competition outside. The CEO told them, this must stop now, or he would have an important decision to make. Chris did the maths and recognised the pressure was on him to turn the volume down on his cynicism. The culture work was something the CEO clearly wanted to happen. For the sake of the team, Chris and Pip agreed to spend some time together to really hear each other out. They both needed to understand where the other was coming from.

Interestingly, both expressed how they had felt judged by the other, which had invoked a defensive and guarded energy between them. The fact that they shared something in common, *the feeling of being judged by the other*, gave them both reason to pause, even invoking a slight chuckle over finally finding something they could agree on. The tension between them was real.

To structure their conversation, the CEO suggested they use a model that he had been introduced to in a leadership programme a few years back.

The model encourages two people who may be in conflict to start the conversation with recognition that both have legitimate needs and concerns in relation to the issue to be solved. Once they agree on the issue, the model calls for each to hear each other's needs and concerns, listening to learn rather than refute, each taking the time to really understand where the other is coming from, not just pretending to. The 'give and take' shifts the dynamic from clash of the titans to both acknowledging the passion they share for the same goal, which is for the business to succeed. Chris and Pip both wanted that. For the first time in their dynamic, no one had to be right or wrong, good or bad, the winner or loser.

They came to a mutually felt understanding that both agreed needed to be co-owned by their respective teams. Chris would support the culture initiative with genuine commitment if Pip agreed to relax the pressures around deadlines and time required in workshops, which often competed and clashed with the Sales operational cadence.

Pip began to understand some of Chris's pressures, to hear him properly for the first time. In her initial month, she had drawn the conclusion that Chris was 'old school' and rigid, unable to understand what the engagement research was all about. Now, in genuine conversations with him, she was pleasantly surprised to learn that he actually knew a thing or two about culture. Chris appreciated that he was finally being heard, rather than judged. He conceded that he had a hard and off-putting edge toward the HR team, which his sales team had mirrored. He accepted that he hadn't exactly modelled one of the company's core values — to work through conflict with above-the-line behaviour. He knew he could set a better example for his team.

This case story reinforces the power of collaboration, which is about suspending ego, status and pride, in the interest of achieving a goal we all agree is more important than any one of us.

True collaboration entails cognitive empathy — to understand, without judgement, where another person is coming from.

Case Story 3:
He Who Doesn't Suffer Fools

This is a story about Tom Hartman, a senior partner in a law firm who runs a leading practice in employment law. Oddly enough, even as an employment lawyer, Tom's team had put up with him bragging for years about how he 'doesn't suffer fools gladly'. There was always some irony between him advising clients on how to mitigate risk associated with poor behaviour, yet he had failed to recognise, for over two decades, what other people saw in him. He took great pride in tearing the skin off opponents, his peers and especially the younger associates who worked for him. After all, that was how he was taught and coached, right through to partner, so he took his success as validation for replicating a coaching style that qualified as bullying on many fronts.

Several talented junior associates had left the firm over the previous year, directly correlated with negative experiences with Tom. The firm's Chair acknowledged the trend as alarming and, on advice from their Director of People & Culture, asked Tom to work with a leadership coach to focus on how to motivate and retain junior talent in the firm. One of the associates who recently departed had threatened to levy a bullying complaint against the firm. The Chair was able to avoid that outcome with the promise that she would do something tangible to intervene. She made it clear to Tom that working with a coach was not optional. The firm could not afford to lose any more talented associates from his team. Something had to change.

Initially, Tom decided to 'play the game' as a way to make some of the noise around him go away. For the first time in his career, there was a negative spotlight on his head. He had no strategy for how to climb out of this hole. He had never before been required to defend his behaviour or change his ways.

Tom's work with the leadership coach entailed collecting feedback on the impact of his leadership. He had never been through a feedback process before. He never anticipated it would be as daunting and confronting as it was. For the first time in his professional career, Tom got to see himself through the eyes of key stakeholders around him. When the feedback rolled in, it wasn't a pretty picture. In fact, it was pretty ugly.

In the span of a very long week, Tom went through the typical 'SARAH' feedback reaction, an acronym for *Shock, Anger, Rejection, Acceptance, Help*. Tom was initially *shocked* by the feedback, especially in learning that many people would walk a mile out of their way to avoid him on a day when he was in his best mood. That really grabbed his attention. He knew that he was tough, but he always thought that was part of being a good leader. For people to want to avoid him really sent him inward, so much so that he couldn't re-read the report in the first three days. That's how confronting the feedback was.

Another partner noticed that Tom had been sulking and enquired about whether he was *angry or upset* about something. He most certainly was angry, feeling betrayed by the people he trusted the most to reflect through their feedback how much they valued him. Well, that certainly didn't happen.

> He had never been through a feedback process before. He never anticipated it would be as daunting and confronting as it was. For the first time in his professional career, Tom got to see himself through the eyes of key stakeholders around him.

Predictably, Tom looked for reasons to *reject* the key themes in the report, wondering if the strain of a very heavy workload over the past quarter might have influenced the negative feedback, something he might then rationalise as 'situational'. That theory certainly died on the vine when his wife finally confronted him about his bad mood. Tom told her about the whole feedback process, stemming from his Chair's concern that he was chasing away talented junior associates. His wife read the feedback report and decided it was time to sit down with Tom and tell him what no one else would probably ever say without anonymity. She told him that she agreed with the themes in the report and would not let him reject the results as situational, nor to rationalise the pain away. What really got his attention was when she told him that their two adult sons had described him the same way. Tom knew he had no comeback. He had reached that same conclusion years ago, something he thought about often. Then she asked him to spend some time thinking about whether he wanted those themes in the feedback to reflect his *legacy* — at the firm and in life. The consistent perception across both spheres was that he was a real jerk. That sunk in very deep.

Reflecting on the conversation with his wife, and three days prior to his next coaching session, Tom read the report again, slower this time, and let the key themes sink in even more. He came to *accept* that the words on the page were really a reflection of who he was. In his heart of hearts, he knew that his wife was right. His legacy was one of bullying and intimidation, the exact opposite of his intent to be revered and respected.

Tom's next session with the leadership coach was different from the first two, when he was there to tick the box and get through the process. He needed *help* to get on top of this scenario, not just to make the noise go away, but to de-Scrooge himself in a major way. Tom had been known for saying 'you can't teach an old dog new tricks.' On the other side of SARAH, he was now ready to learn some new tricks, not to make the noise go away, but to re-think what it meant to be respected. When Tom was a junior associate, one of the firm's partners repeatedly pronounced, 'It's more important to be respected than liked.' Tom had adopted that mentality as his own. Now he reflected deeply to consider how many people he truly respected, yet didn't like, over his career. He struggled to think of a single person.

Tom had no idea that he had closed his mind to hearing new ways of thinking about age-old challenges in the legal world. In their exit interviews, the associates who left his team over the past year had all cited as their top reason Tom's 'unwillingness to hear their views

In their exit interviews, the associates who left his team over the past year had all cited as their top reason Tom's 'unwillingness to hear their views and suggestions'.

and suggestions'. For him, learning had been one-way directionally — from him to them. The less-than-subtle message to his team was *I do the thinking, you do the doing.* For Gen Y and Z employees under the age of 35, a huge part of engagement is being able to bring their perspective to the table, to be able to learn by contributing. They know the manager will make the decision, but they appreciate feeling a part of the outcome.

Over the next couple of weeks, Tom scanned the internet for articles and podcasts about staff and team engagement. This was new territory for him, having never attended a formal leadership development programme before. What was previously the 'soft stuff' was now becoming tangible and real for him. He learned the formal definitions of staff engagement, as well as what drives it. The common theme was *listening*, where people feel like their perspective matters in a decision. Ask people their opinion, then listen. Easier said than done for most of his life, but now it really mattered.

One month after receiving the feedback, Tom called a meeting of his broader team to talk about how they might reconfigure the last half of their weekly meeting agenda to have more open-ended conversations about common challenges they were all facing. For him to be more engaged with his team, it would require him to do less talking and far more listening. He had to practise really hard not to interrupt, but he was making progress.

Tom knew that it would take some time to win the team's trust and to open up some positive energy across their dynamic. And he understood why this was the case. His wife's perspective on legacy really got his attention. It resonated with him deep in his heart. He could not believe that he had used the word 'fool' to describe people on his team he apparently would not suffer gladly, whatever the heck that meant. Be tough on those more junior to you. Kiss up and kick down. That's how he was raised. He was never close with his dad and he knew the very same scenario was now unfolding with his sons. On top of that, the youngest members of his team had departed over the past year. Tom knew he was the common denominator on both fronts. Over the past month, his mental models about leadership began to shift big time. One thing was for sure, he would never say the word 'fool' again. There were no fools on his team.

COGNITIVE EMPATHY
KEY THEMES FROM THE CASE STORIES

1. Share Perspective

In Emirhan's story, Cheryl took time with her new peers to suggest they consider what it would be like if the team suddenly decided what their name would be, without them having a vote, and to consider that decision from Emirhan's perspective.

With Tom Hartman's story, his wife brought him some much-needed candour mixed with empathy, knocking him solidly between the eyes with the hard reality that he should lose the word 'fool' from his vocabulary forever.

2. Suspend Judgement

With Chris and Pip, both finally shared their feelings and concerns about the other and their teams, which included surfacing assumptions about motive and intent. Both laughed at how divisive those assumptions had become over the past year, resolved by a long overdue conversation.

Looping back to Tom Hartman, it took him nearly a week to reflect on the feedback report he received without trying to reject or dismiss it. After the conversation with his wife, he went into a considered and reflective mindset, the most prevalent question being, 'Am I closed to feedback?'

3. Curiosity and Learning

In the three stories, curiosity was a source of connecting energy. Emirhan really appreciated how Cheryl put the conversation on the table with the team in such a way that did not come across as judging them, but rather as pointing out an unconscious bias where we ask people to fit in with the norm, even if it means compromising who they are. Cheryl's empathy for them made it much easier for her peers to show the same to Emirhan. With cognitive empathy, you judge people less.

With Chris and Pip, they had to change the dynamic between them and their teams very quickly. Their CEO gave them no choice. So, it could have been a matter of which of us folds first, or should we look at this as an opportunity to open up the energy between us? Thankfully, they got to a better place, to hear each other without judgement, to land on a good spot. Yes, it is possible for both people to be right.

After the feedback, Tom grew more eager to hear views from team members who were 30 years his junior. They all knew he was still the boss, but now everyone felt more comfortable to express a view on important decisions rather than sitting quietly. For Tom, that meant listening with a different ear.

Conversation Boosters

Here are some ways to navigate your way into or through a conversation where cognitive empathy can make a big difference.

Cognitive Empathy Mindset

- Imagine yourself going through the same thought process as the other person to land on a position or view that they hold.
- Unless a moral, ethical or legal principle has been breached, keep your mind open to where the person is coming from, even if you disagree.
- Suspend judgement and appraisal. Listen to learn rather than to refute.
- Recall a time when you didn't believe that someone was making a genuine effort to hear you out. What would have made a positive difference for you then? Can you show that to another person now?
- Pay attention to when emotions overrule your ability to listen and really hear another person. Why are certain things 'hot buttons' for you?

What Not to Say

How can you possibly believe that?

I have no idea what you are talking about.

You're being irrational.

You sound like a broken record.

Can you please just get with the programme?

We agree to disagree.

What to Say

I'm following your logic, please continue.

I can understand why you feel that way.

You're in a tough spot here.

Wow, that sounds terrible.

I can see how you landed on that position.

I agree with several of your points and here's why. And here's where we disagree.

No wonder you're upset.

I would have trouble coping with that too.

Landing with Impact

Thanks for taking me through your thinking to understand your position better. Based on that, here is where I stand.

That sounds like a tough predicament you are in. Let me know how I can help.

I can't relate personally to what you have experienced, but I imagine it must be really tough.

We clearly disagree on the best way to resolve this, but I appreciate that we want the same outcome.

9

EMOTIONAL EMPATHY: THREE CASE STORIES

DEFINITION
When you physically and instinctively feel for, and along with, the other person going through an experience, almost as if their emotions are contagious.

WHAT IT ENTAILS
Feelings, physical sensations, putting yourself there in the moment through mirror neurons in the brain.

BENEFITS
- Helps in building close interpersonal relationships.
- An asset in careers such as team leadership, coaching, marketing and people/culture.

PITFALLS
- Can be overwhelming or all-consuming if objectivity is lost.
- Potentially inappropriate in certain relationship or chain-of-command circumstances.

Case Story 4: All in This Together

This case story was very real for many people in a pandemic year like 2020 when livelihoods were put on hold or slipped away from them permanently. Like many companies, a decent-sized and profitable insurance business had to rapidly restructure and downsize the team that sold travel insurance — no other choice, really — in a year when countries' borders were closed and people couldn't travel abroad without significant consequences. Profitability had dropped 70 per cent compared with the team's performance at that same time a year earlier.

The marketing manager, Brad, knew that the business would have to downsize staff by 50 per cent, roughly 35 people. That included job losses on the leadership team and right down through each of their teams. Brad had seven people who reported to him, two of whom had only joined the business earlier that year, with no idea how much they would regret leaving other jobs to come on board. The COVID-19 scenario rocked many people's worlds in the same way.

Brad could feel the anxiety build and grow every day through a drawn-out two-week process, which was daunting for his team. At the time, he reflected on how he had never before faced anything of this magnitude in his life. Not only a global pandemic with no playbook, but also having to keep a team focused and positive. Yet, even with his own angst, magnified by that of his team, Brad felt very connected to them, and they to him, in a way he never anticipated.

This was different from all the previous restructures Brad had led or been part of in his career — five in total. On each of those previous occasions, he was advised early on that his job would not be impacted. That made things difficult for him because he often felt, in conversations with his team, like he was being disingenuous, reading from a prepared script written by HR. In those earlier restructures, Brad preferred the very strong emphasis on process. By following the required process, this meant that he was forbidden to have 'off-the-record' conversations with any staff who might lose their jobs in the downsizing. This was a relief to him because he dreaded that awful look in their eyes, trying to keep them focused and positive when they all knew he couldn't possibly relate to what they were going through.

Vulnerability is the feeling of exposure associated with imperfection. Brad felt very exposed as an imperfect manager during each of the previous restructures. He hated being part of the disruption that upset so many people's lives, unable to do anything tangible to help them. Hiding behind the prepared script in neatly sequenced conversations was a safe place to hide. He felt less guilt there. His job was always spared.

This time around, things were very different. In a bizarre sort of way, it was almost a 'freeing' experience for Brad. In a year when anxiety for most people was at an all-time high, he felt a sense of liberation going through that seismic restructure. For the first time ever and, particularly as a manager, he was just as vulnerable as everyone else around him. For the first time, he could look his team in the eye and relate to that worried look staring back at him. For the first time, he was not guided by a prepared script to be delivered in rote fashion on a particular date. He encouraged his team to stay positive and to keep things in proper perspective. And he meant it, fuelled by the fact that, for the first time, he had to take his own advice. And the team knew it.

Now Brad was going through the same experience as everyone else. He could feel the connection with his team. It was palpable. All their fates were being determined by the CEO within a tight inner circle, along with board oversight. This was a decision completely beyond their control. Most of the team had been here before; a restructure is never easy to go through. But it was easier to get through one when other people around you knew what it felt like, what it was like to be on the receiving end of a prepared script. They felt a more direct connection through their shared vulnerability, not having the answers, dealing with uncertainty, dependent on decision makers who weren't sharing much information, not being able to predict how the

For the first time ever and, particularly as a manager, he was just as vulnerable as everyone else around him.

rest of the year would play out. For Brad, it was like someone turned on a light switch for him. He finally saw that vulnerability entails a fair dose of self-compassion — being okay with not knowing the answer or not being able to fix a problem for someone. The connection he felt with his team was liberating. He was genuinely positive as he encouraged his team to keep the faith.

As Brad predicted and prepared himself to hear, his role was made redundant, along with three members of his team of seven. In the new structure, three of the roles on his team would shift to a different team. All those who were made redundant were invited to contend for new roles, but several, including Brad, decided that it was time for a new chapter in their lives.

Brad felt the new roles were more junior to where he had operated over the past few years. Even in the face of an economic downturn with direct impact on the number of available roles in the market, he felt confident about his decision to stay focused on an upward trajectory in his career. Brad and his wife had discussed the decision for nearly three months. In fact, they grew closer because of it. A fortnight later, Brad departed, along with many others who were impacted by the downsizing.

Over the next few months, Brad stayed in touch with members of his team who had also exited the business. He had come to think of them as friends rather than former direct reports. Their shared vulnerability levelled the playing field. They were benefiting from each other's support, well-wishes and networks. Brad was helpful in connecting several of them with recruitment firms that could be of help. And Brad benefitted from an introduction by one of his former team members to meet with the marketing director of a former competitor.

Near the six-month anniversary of his departure, Brad received a HUGE hand-made 'thank you' card, signed by every single person on his former team about the impact his leadership had on their ability to navigate, with greater confidence, through such an anxious time in their lives. Brad was touched by the gift, which reinforced his new insights about the power of vulnerability. As a starting point, people don't need you to fix anything for them. They just need to feel understood. The connection is deeper if you have actually walked in their shoes, which he had certainly done. Brad's story is a relevant and timely example of emotional empathy. The ability to feel with someone is often the only support they ever need from you.

Case Story 5:
A Common Bond

What unites two people is often much stronger than what divides them. This is a story about two 'rivals' at work, Steve and Simon, who had long put up with one  another, neither investing much of anything in a personal connection between them. The rivalry had largely been around pride and status. Both guys ran different businesses under an iconic brand portfolio. These two guys met up six times annually with their board's chair, along with two of their other peers, where they tried to align around best practice and how best to drive efficiencies across the businesses. Other than those six meetings each year, they rarely interacted with each other. Most people saw them as competitors who did not care much for the other, perpetuated by their own lack of discretion in conversations with other people.

What connected the two? Steve learned from the Chair that Simon's wife, Barb, had been diagnosed with breast cancer. Simon had not come into the office over the past week, working from home and mostly unplugged, trying to be fully present with Barb. Word rippled quickly across the broader group that he was working through a tough life scenario with his wife.

After hearing about Barb's cancer, Steve told his wife, Vonn, who had survived breast cancer eight years earlier when she was 42. Vonn was immediately grabbed by the essence of what Barb would be going through. She and Barb had met twice previously at company functions, enough to exchange a warm hello, but always seemingly on the other side of the table where neither could strike up a proper conversation.

Vonn insisted to Steve that they reach out to Simon and Barb. Steve was uncomfortable about this, not sure how to even approach Simon to say 'hang in there.' They didn't have that kind of relationship; never once had either called the other to talk about something other than work. Steve told Vonn he was pretty sure Simon and Barb had three grown kids, although he wasn't certain. That is how little he knew about Simon. Vonn persisted that Steve call Simon. She had some personal insights she wanted to share with Barb, things she wished someone would have shared with her when she was preparing to face the battle for her life. Vonn would not let it go, so Steve finally picked up the phone and called Simon.

Vonn grabbed the phone out of Steve's hand after she sensed he was stuck within 90 seconds of saying hello to Simon. She expressed her heartfelt empathy and support for what they were both going through, then asked if there might be an opportune time for a quick conversation with Barb; she wanted to pass along some thoughts that might make a difference in her battle with breast cancer. This had been a part of Vonn's WHY since winning her own battle, to help make a difference for women who feared the worst and were inclined to go inward with those fears. Simon thanked Vonn and said he would talk with Barb and come back to her. Vonn suggested they could connect virtually if that was easier for Barb. Simon was touched by Vonn's warmth and her kindness to reach out to Barb. That evening, he told Barb about the conversation and she graciously accepted Vonn's outreach. They didn't know each other well, but she had enjoyed their brief exchanges at company functions. She asked Simon to call Steve and arrange for a virtual call the next day.

The two couples met up on a Zoom call the following day. Simon and Steve were mostly silent on the call, the conversation being largely between their wives. Vonn had two things she wanted to share with Barb. One was a cake that she had baked that morning for their family. It turned out Simon was wrong about how many kids they had, two rather than three, and both had returned home to be with their mum during such a difficult time. The second gift was a small seedling, freshly transplanted into a sizeable and colourful planter shaped as a hand. The planter had special significance to Vonn when she went through her cancer treatments eight years earlier. She talked about the metamorphosis of a new plant in rich soil, synchronised with her own recovery. Vonn told Barb she had kept her focus on that seedling every day for several weeks as she recovered, and how it helped her to keep things in proper perspective. Barb was really touched by both gifts. Vonn arranged for the cake and planter to be delivered the same day.

Two hours after their Zoom call, Steve was in deep thought over what Simon would be going through at the moment. So, he picked up the phone and called his peer, the first time ever for something totally unrelated to work. He told Simon he had been thinking about how he navigated through the same scenario eight years earlier. He reflected on how he felt back then, a powerful man who was rendered powerless in Vonn's battle with cancer, unable to use wealth or power or influence to make the pain and fear go away for her. Steve advised Simon to focus on 'being there', to really be there, for Barb and their two sons, both very anxious over the prospect of losing their mother.

> *He reflected on how he felt back then, a powerful man who was rendered powerless in Vonn's battle with cancer, unable to use wealth or power or influence to make the pain and fear go away for her.*

Steve said that, through his own sense of helplessness when he realised his clout could not help Vonn with her battle, he learned an invaluable lesson about what 'support' really means for most people. When he could not fix the problem with wealth or influence, he realised his only power was in giving fully of himself — to just be there, emotionally available, unplugged and present.

Simon thanked Steve for sharing those words of advice. He had recognised those very feelings within his own myriad of emotions over the previous 10 days. With Barb's mastectomy scheduled in 48 hours, he could definitely relate to the sentiment, that same sense of helplessness, the same vulnerability associated with having to surrender control to the unknown. Simon wasn't a spiritual guy by any means, but he had prayed for help a few times over the past week. He shared this with Steve, who said he could relate because he had done the same when Vonn battled cancer. Both chuckled about how their conversations with God had always been around scenarios like this, where they felt helpless. Before they ended the call, Simon thanked Steve again for calling, both with Vonn and then separately. It really meant a lot to him.

That very gesture of support, one couple to the other, had enhanced the connection between Simon and Steve, as well as with their partners. Steve called Simon weekly over the next five weeks to inquire about Barb's recovery and to see how he was tracking. Vonn and Barb had also connected virtually twice since then, to talk about her recovery. Over the next six months, the dynamic between both couples grew noticeably stronger. They all had connected through their respective bouts with vulnerability, where the only thing they could do to help anyone was simply to 'be there'.

This case story reinforces three points. The first is that common challenges in life tend to break down walls between people. At the end of the day, prime ministers and homeless people face the same challenges on occasions. Secondly, to give of your authentic self makes it easier for others to do the same. Steve reaching out to Simon to discuss their respective bouts with vulnerability was connecting for both. Thirdly, quality definitely prevails over quantity in the broader scheme of life. These two business rivals learned that life is not about winning or losing, but about living. Simon and Steve still differed on fundamental business principles, but it no longer felt 'personal' for either of them. That is the real impact of emotional empathy. People really do appreciate your support when it comes from the heart.

Case Story 6:
The Fine Line

This is a case story about an entrepreneur, Meghan, who learned, the hard way about the fine line that separates emotional empathy from emotional contagion. It is termed 'countertransference' in psychotherapy, where the therapist takes on the symptoms of the patient and loses objectivity. This same thing happens for many people in their efforts to 'be there' for someone else. It is the same as wearing someone's pain for them.

Meg was the manager of a fitness centre under her own brand, which had been her dream since the age of 15. At 40, her dream had evolved from a concept to a very real thing. Slowly but steadily across their first 18 months, the business began to turn a profit. She had a team of three trainers who had started to build up their own client base. All the markers for success were in place. Meg relished being her own boss and doing something that made a positive difference for people. She believed that she had tapped into something she loved doing, a clear sense of purpose that was having real impact on the lives of others.

One of her trainers, Felicity, who had been on board with Meg since the first day, started to dive into a melancholy space, linked on the surface to what seemed like an abusive relationship, but anchored more around a recurring pattern of depression. Over the past three months, Felicity's waning energy had become more apparent. It started to impact on her ability to deliver on her commitments, especially when she had to cancel classes and her client base started to dwindle because of her unreliability.

Meg felt she could relate to what Felicity was going through and hoped that this would make it easier for her to accept advice and support from someone who had been there. Twenty years earlier, Meg experienced a bout of depression, while also entrapped in an unhealthy relationship — a not uncommon cycle. Meg's then-boyfriend changed the instant they decided to move in together, a move she would come to regret. She struggled in the relationship for 18 months, then backed herself to end it and put it behind her as quickly as possible. At 22, Meg had learned a valuable insight about how to live her life. If you can't respect yourself, is it reasonable to expect others to do so? The same spirit eventually shaped itself into a dream come true for Meg, one that she was now living every day. Her fitness business was about uplifting the quality of life for clients.

Now, this scenario with her employee was conjuring up memories of her own struggles in that dysfunctional relationship, more vividly than she had anticipated. Meg started to reflect and ponder deeply about how she managed to rationalise the abuse as 'normal' for nearly two years back then. She recalled feeling judged by people who were trying to be supportive, perhaps not with the right words, but the best of intentions. She always felt on the back foot, in a defensive posture with family and friends, trying to justify why she would put up with something like that. She couldn't recall feeling much empathy coming from her family and friends at the time, which fuelled her strategy to put it all behind her as quickly as possible.

Meg wanted Felicity to have a different experience, to feel the support and to know that someone understood what she was going through. She went out of her way to show support for her, including the offer for Felicity to move into her home temporarily if she felt unsafe with her boyfriend. Felicity found that to be a bit presumptive and graciously declined Meg's offer to flat with her.

She couldn't recall feeling much empathy coming from her family and friends at the time, which fuelled her strategy to put it all behind her as quickly as possible.

Over the next couple weeks, Meg started to go overboard with her support for Felicity — doing things for her in a way that felt disempowering, that very same feeling you have when someone shows their support through excessive doses of pity. Ironically, the effort to show you care can start to feel less like empathy and more like being pitied, akin to being judged for not having your act together. In the moment, Meg could not fully appreciate that Felicity was feeling the same way she had 20 years earlier when people were pitying her.

It all started to flow over when Meg encouraged Felicity to take some time off if she needed the space; she and the other two trainers would step in and fill the gap. As predicted, the load started to increase on the other two trainers with no extra compensation to boot. That didn't go down well with either of them, who could understand what Felicity was going through, but were not willing to absorb extra work for no compensation. Their view was that Felicity was a grown woman who now had to make some tough calls, including whether the job suited her anymore. The two trainers worked up the courage to raise their concerns with Meg, who had not seen it coming. They told her it didn't seem fair to ask them to pick up the load associated with Felicity's personal scenario, particularly if there was no long-term solution in place. They were not prepared to wait it out until things improved with Felicity. They wanted a more viable short-term solution.

While all of this was brewing, Meg started to send Felicity various

> It is important for leaders to be extra mindful of the possibility that they can be triggered and drawn into another person's struggle, based on a similar experience they once had in their own lives.

articles and TED Talks on how to get unstuck from a bad relationship, how to combat depression, and so on. The final straw was when Meg sent Felicity an email strongly encouraging her to consider a protective order against her partner and offering to connect her with a prominent attorney in town who could make things happen quickly should she choose to go down the divorce path.

Meg had clearly started to wear Felicity's pain personally and the lines started to blur between which one of them was solving the problem. From Felicity's vantage point, Meg's concern felt intrusive. Leaders with a heart are often faced with the challenge of knowing where that fine line is, and not crossing it.

It is important for leaders to be extra mindful of the possibility that they can be triggered and drawn into another person's struggle, based on a similar experience they once had in their own lives. It is almost like they get a chance for a do-over, except they are living the experience vicariously through another person. This is all under-the-surface stuff, subliminal to the person as they try to be supportive. As was the case with Meg, a person experiencing emotional contagion started to pressure the other person to do all the things they wished they had done for themselves. Even with the best of intentions, this can feel intrusive, certainly disempowering, for the recipient.

Two days after Meg's email about the attorney, Felicity submitted her resignation, having already started to look for work elsewhere. She told Meg that, while she appreciated all the support she had given her over the past month, it had started to become a bit awkward with the sole focus in all their interactions being on her personal life, rather than on the business. With all the undue attention, she had started to feel a bit self-conscious around the other two trainers, like she wasn't pulling her weight. The final straw was Meg's suggestion that she seek a protection order against her husband. Felicity had been reluctant to tell Meg that she and her husband were actually on a reconciliation path, fearing the news might have actually offended, or even disappointed Meg in some way.

A leader's tendency to immerse too deeply into another person's pain, often fuelled by similar experiences in their own life, must not cross over that essential boundary between 'feeling with' another person and wearing their pain for them. With the latter, you are prone to lose your objective lens around issues pertinent to performance management. If you go overboard to show support without holding people accountable for performance, it can have a negative impact on team morale and perceptions of your leadership.

EMOTIONAL EMPATHY
KEY THEMES FROM THE CASE STORIES

1. A Visceral Connection

Brad was mindful of how going through the same experience with the team helped him to be more genuine in his conversations and with his support. The stronger connection stoked his own personal energy, even as he faced a huge cloud of uncertainty himself.

Steve thought long and hard about what Simon must be going through. In similar shoes, he never had a conversation about how helpless he felt as an executive with considerable influence, yet he could do absolutely nothing other than be there with his wife. This is what he wanted to tell Simon. Just be there with Barb.

Meg definitely felt a strong connection with Felicity, having gone through a similar experience in a bad relationship earlier in life. The important lesson here is that she should not let the anxiety push her into the zone of taking control, which is neither required nor ideal when it comes to emotional empathy.

2. Reflection and Perspective

Brad's perspective on emotional intelligence and the importance of empathy grew tremendously, even as he navigated through the toughest professional and personal scenario in his life. First-hand, he learned what it means to truly be on someone's level, not just in understanding their challenge, but actually experiencing it with them. He never felt closer to a team than when going through the redundancy that impacted them all.

Steve set the example of sharing something deeply personal with Simon because he hoped it would make a difference for someone going through a similar experience. Steve feared that his gesture would be seen as intrusive, perhaps crossing the line. Worn as a strength, vulnerability entitles you to intrude when you sense the other person may be struggling with how to ask for support. Coming from a good place, you will rarely regret doing so.

Following Felicity's departure, Meg reflected on how her efforts to support her team member went into an uncomfortable space, to the point where Felicity started to feel judged, even controlled. This was not Meg's intent, but it led to Felicity's departure. Too much support, delivered with intensity, can be off-putting to people who are capable of doing things for themselves.

3. The Fine Line

Brad did not get close to that line where emotional empathy suddenly turned into a personal cause to rescue his team. He discovered that 'being present' was all people needed, very different from when he once avoided those who were being made redundant because he couldn't rescue them. He wasn't able to fix anything for anyone, yet the connection was palpable.

Steve was able to convey the same insights to Simon, not wanting to be overly intrusive, but wanting to make sure his peer didn't put too much pressure on himself to fix what he couldn't. They both walked that fine line well, now leaning in more as supportive colleagues as opposed to detached workmates.

On the other hand, Meg did cross that line with Felicity. It wasn't intentional, as it rarely is when a person is trying to be supportive. Again, to feel with someone does not require you to wear their pain. It can be very overwhelming and disempowering when this happens. Even if you can feel it, it's important to stay on your side of that fine line.

Conversation Boosters

Here are some ways to navigate your way into or through a conversation where emotional empathy can make a big difference.

Emotional Empathy Mindset

- Based on a similar experience in life, you can personally relate to what the person is going through. Your sentiment is heart-felt.
- Be an anchor in the conversation. Stay grounded when the emotions start to swirl around in your own mind. This is the other person's experience in the here and now, so avoid going insular.
- Stay connected through nods, affirmation and being fully present. Tears or anger are okay if that is how you feel.
- Let the person talk, feel and own the space as they work their way through myriad emotions. Less voice, more ears.
- Never tell someone how they should feel about something they are going through. Just let them talk about how they feel.
- Try not to replay or rewrite your history through the person's experience. This is their scenario to work through, not yours.

What Not to Say

How can you possibly feel that way?

C'mon, suck it up and get over it already.

I don't care about feelings or intuition, just talk to me about the facts.

I thought you were stronger than this.

Been there, done that, now move on.

I was able to work my way through it. Why can't you?

What to Say

How can I be helpful to you?

It hurts me to hear what you have to deal with.

From personal experience, I know what you're going through.

No wonder you're upset. I can relate.

I have felt the same way you do in your situation.

It's okay to feel frustrated. But please don't beat yourself up too much over what happened.

Landing with Impact

I once worked my way through the same scenario and learned from it. I am confident that you will too.

I can tell you what worked for me, but the reality is that you will have to find your way through this situation one step at a time. Call on me if you need a sounding board.

Please don't apologise for how you feel. It's a very human thing to feel the way you do right now.

I may not be the most objective person to talk with about this, so you may want to share your thinking with a few other people to get their views too.

I'm accessible if you need to talk, so please don't hesitate to call. I'm happy to lend an ear.

10

COMPASSIONATE EMPATHY: THREE CASE STORIES

DEFINITION

This kind of empathy not only enables you to understand another person's predicament and feel with them, but you are spontaneously moved to help, if needed.

WHAT IT ENTAILS
- Intellect
- Emotional connection
- Action

BENEFITS
- Your perspective considers the whole person
- Making a difference in a way that matters

PITFALLS
- Very few
- Compassion is often considered the mode of empathy with the biggest impact, but be aware of sociopaths who exploit kindness.

Case Story 7:
The Newcomer

Andy, the newest member to the team, was struggling to find his voice. He had joined the business at a time when financial pressures had started to mount, requiring the team to make some tough choices about what remained a priority and what should be parked or shut down altogether. With these tough choices came mounting tensions around the table. In these discussions, Andy was coming across as timid, seemingly daunted. He had been promoted to the team after his manager left suddenly, which created the opportunity for him to step up. He knew that his manager had hired him as his likely successor, but he never anticipated it would happen as quickly as it did. Two weeks ago, Andy had been in his zone — confident and fully engaged around the role he had joined the company for, just eight months earlier. In one crazy fortnight, his world had changed dramatically. He was now at the lead table, facing a tough scenario of the business underperforming, and his confidence was missing in action.

Andy had no clue about impostor syndrome and how common it is, so he fought back the nagging feeling that he was unqualified to be at the table. He could literally feel his heart racing as he sat there hoping that none of his new colleagues would ask him a question about his part of the business. He didn't know the whole patch that he had inherited yet, just the part he had been brought in to run. This had never happened to him before, where he was thrust into a bigger role within the blink of an eye. It had been a long time since Andy had experienced anxiety at this level. Talk about vulnerability — he was certainly there and hoped he was hiding it well.

One of Andy's peers on the team, Mark, could see what was happening. They didn't know each other well at all, but Mark could feel what the newest member was going through. He had been there before himself. In fact, he was also brought onto the team under very similar circumstances two years earlier. Mark was a communications expert and had joined the company to run a very specific function to help improve relationships with external stakeholders. The manager who hired him had been with the company for 21 years, mostly as head of corporate services. Mark learned of his former boss's departure only four weeks before he left, with a similar tap on the shoulder as Andy's, to step up into a bigger role at the lead table. Fortunately, Mark had worked in the same industry for nearly a decade, so he knew his way around a bit with the language and felt that he could hold his own in a high-level conversation. But now watching Andy struggle to get his footing, he recalled his own struggles and the same dread that someone would call him out as an impostor.

Impostor syndrome is a common set of thoughts and feelings, experienced by roughly 75 per cent of people who raise their hand or are tapped on the shoulder to take on a bigger role. Even while common, especially in the workplace, most people going through impostor syndrome are reluctant to talk about it, fearing they will stand out as inadequate because no one else can possibly relate to their experience. It is an intriguing paradox, one that speaks to the impact of vulnerability on people when it is largely misunderstood. When going through impostor syndrome, people usually inflate or deflate their persona as a way to ward off threat. Making your persona smaller means that you are less of a target. Making your persona larger also wards off threat, especially if you have the gift of the gab. Either way, smaller or larger, it is difficult to connect with someone who is likely to see your efforts to help as a sign of weakness on their part.

Mark knew that Andy would be trying to make this all work in his mind via the path of least resistance. If you don't talk about it, it doesn't exist.

Mark carefully considered how to offer Andy his support. He was reluctant to put Andy on the spot to talk about feelings of inadequacy or his struggles to fit in with the team. He didn't know Andy that well and thought it might come across as intrusive and offensive if he requested a meeting to talk about how terrified he must be. From his own experience, he knew that denial is a dear friend of impostor syndrome. Mark knew that Andy would be trying to make this all work in his mind via the path of least resistance.

If you don't talk about it, it doesn't exist. That was how he had felt two years earlier. Yet, he could see the anxiety in Andy's eyes and hear it in his voice. He seemed really lost in his new position and Mark wanted to do something to help.

The opportunity unfolded at their next board meeting, where three of the seven team members were scheduled to present their results. That month's board rotation just so happened to include both Mark and Andy, so Mark saw an opportunity to approach Andy. He invited him to lunch to offer up some perspective on the board — who was who, who to suck up to, who to avoid, who to spend extra time with. Andy was very impressed with Mark's intuition for how to connect best with each board member.

More importantly, Mark laid out for Andy how best to unpack his presentation on the day, very similar advice that Andy had already received from the CEO. But Mark went into more intricate and intimate detail on how to connect with each member — those points to reinforce, those to avoid, and how to play to one specific board member who was not savvy with metrics and preferred that the presenter paint a verbal picture for him instead. So, Mark spent more time with Andy a couple of days later, helping him to come up with a game plan of where his team was going over the next year. For Andy, this was an invaluable act of compassion on the part of his peer, who he had hardly known one month earlier, but had quickly become a confidant in a matter of 48 hours.

Andy's presentation to the board went reasonably well, albeit with a few hiccups and awkward pauses along the way. But the general feedback was that the new guy was pretty impressive and a good choice to fill his old boss's role. Mark was not in the room when Andy gave his presentation, so he was waiting in another conference room, hoping that things had gone well for his new peer. They gave each other a high five when Andy walked in with a big grin on his face. Andy said to Mark, 'I owe you a dozen drinks, all tonight if you prefer.' They both laughed and headed back to join the rest of the team for a final wrap up with the board.

That boost of confidence was huge for Andy, who started to find his voice at the table within four weeks. Following the positive feedback from the board, he began to bring his views with greater confidence, thanks to the coaching of Mark, who had given him constructive advice along the way. Mark felt good about reaching out to his new peer and helping to take the impostor monkey off his back. His act of compassion was manifest through explicit actions to reach out and support Andy up the learning curve as quickly as possible.

It is important to recognise that compassionate empathy runs two ways. Empathy is not only about being able to give of yourself to others in a way that matters. As was the case with Andy, empathy is also about being able to receive compassion from others, especially to recognise how someone has put themselves out to go the extra mile for you. Having strong EQ is not only about being able to give. It is also about being able to receive. In the middle between the two, there is real connection.

Case Story 8:
Leadership is Larger than Rank

Lieutenant General David Morrison, former Commander of Australia's army and Australian of the Year in 2015, famously told his troops in the face of systemic sexual harassment of female soldiers, 'the standard you walk by is the standard you accept.' That ethos comes through in the story of Theo, the youngest (21) and least experienced guy on the team in a small agribusiness plant. In one key moment, Theo went from having no mana to significant mana through the power of his character. His story is a lot like Emirhan's colleague, Cheryl, who requested that their peers call him by his given Turkish name. Empathy is often shown through interventions people make on behalf of others anonymously. Theo did that very thing on behalf of his new colleague, Sandra, who had joined the team a month earlier. She just so happened to be the only woman on the team, which came into play.

Whenever Sandra left the room, the six guys found a way, each and every time, to make less-than-subtle innuendos and poorly veiled references about how she was not going to work out. One guy actually said several times that she must be 'on the rag'. Initially, Theo laughed along with their antics, trying to fit in as one of the boys, wanting very much to be liked by the two oldest members, Oli and Bart, who were twice his age and very good at their jobs. In his first full year on the team, Theo had learned a lot from them both. But he didn't like the dynamic that had evolved over the month since Sandra joined the team. He started to feel uncomfortable with some of the things the guys were saying about her, but he continued to smile and sit quietly, no longer laughing out loud.

Over the past week, Theo and Sandra had run into each other twice at a local café, just down the road from the plant where they worked. On that second day, they sat down and had a coffee together. Sandra took a chance and confided in him about how she had been feeling since joining the team. Sandra said she felt a disconnect every time she walked into the room. She thanked Theo for making time to have a coffee. Theo liked Sandra and told her not to read too much into anything. He said, 'the guys are typically grumpy and walk around with their heads down all day.' He told her not to take it personally, although he knew her intuition had picked up on something that was very real.

He started to feel uncomfortable with some of the things the guys were saying about her, but he continued to smile and sit quietly, no longer laughing out loud.

Three days later, Sandra left the main area and the guys turned on her, mocking her, laughing about a mistake she had made, sounding like six hyenas circling around each other. That was when Theo started to feel sick to his stomach. The nausea hit him like a tonne of bricks and he could feel the rage building in him. While he was still seated, he pounded the desk and shouted, 'Stop it!' And they all did.

Theo told them he could no longer sit there and take part in something that felt very wrong to him. He had been losing sleep over the last couple weeks as he lay awake pondering that very moment when he would lose his cool. He had predicted to himself it would come to that. And now there he was, in the moment. Theo told the guys about how he had a conversation with Sandra about her concerns that she wasn't fitting in with the team. He told them that he suggested she might be overthinking it, when, all along, he knew her radar was reading the energy accurately. And Theo told them that he was personally offended by the things they had said about her and challenged any of them to laugh if the same were happening to their mother, wife, sister or daughter. He could see that wash over the faces of the six guys who were now standing very quietly, listening to him.

Theo said, 'I get physically sick when you guys do that, and I'm not going to participate in any of these conversations anymore.' With that, his adrenaline shut him down. Trembling, and with his heart palpitating unlike at any other time in his life, he got up and walked out of the room and down the hall to the exit door, where he pushed through to the car park and leaned against the wall to catch his breath. This was a new experience for him. He had never done anything like that before. He felt both liberated and terrified, immediately worried that he had pissed off the guys, especially Oli and Bart, who he had a lot of time and respect for. Or once did.

Compassionate empathy is often shown through courage and taking a stand on something that is important to you.

The story ended in a great space when Oli came out to the car park to find Theo. Oli walked up to him, extended his hand, and said, 'Thanks, man.' Theo looked at the ground and immediately started to apologise. Oli interrupted him and said, 'Thanks for helping us be a better team. We are better than that. Thanks for helping us see it.' Theo took a deep breath. A keen insight was starting to mushroom in his head as Oli spoke. Leadership is not about rank, nor is it about age. It is about bringing your voice and perspective to the table when you believe you can make a difference. This young 21 year old with the lowest rank on the team, and the highest empathy, managed to get their attention and shift the dial on creating a more inclusive team culture for the newest member.

The standard you walk by is the standard you accept. If you reinforce the principle that leadership is not about rank, but about having a perspective, it opens up accountability for everyone to uphold the standard. Compassionate empathy is often shown through courage and taking a stand on something that is important to you. Theo learned a valuable lesson about life on that day when he discovered his voice.

Case Story 9:
Guess Who's Coming to Dinner

This is my story. And the title is a flashback to the famous 1967 movie, starring Sydney Poitier, Spencer Tracy and Katharine Hepburn. Poitier's character, a black man, is dating a white woman, the daughter of Tracy and Hepburn's characters. They all meet up together for the first time over dinner at the family home, engaged in some intriguing conversations as they make their way through the awkwardness of interracial dating. By today's standards on who we choose to date, that movie seems like a thousand years ago. But still, the title is so befitting of the time when I first experienced a deep sense of belonging.

As early as five years old, I knew that I was university-bound, inspired by my father calling me 'Dr Hillman' and stoking a voracious appetite in me and my younger sister for books, even before either of us could read. My father died before my sister and I became authors, but his inspiration is a shining example of how powerful it is to plant a vision in a young kid's head and then let it blossom in their psyche over time. By the time I was in high school, it wasn't a matter of if I would go to university. The question was where.

As early as five years old, I knew that I was university-bound, inspired by my father calling me 'Dr Hillman' and stoking a voracious appetite in me and my younger sister for books, even before either of us could read.

I had several older cousins who were college graduates, a few who became teachers. Growing up in a poor and black neighbourhood didn't lend itself to the best high school to attend in terms of college prep. My older brothers had both attended Spingarn, the neighbourhood high school, which didn't have an impressive percentage of students who went on to attend university. In a New Zealand context, Spingarn would have been a Decile 1 school, focused largely on trade skills, such as woodwork and metalwork for boys and 'home economics' for girls. In my middle school years, a few of my teachers encouraged me to attend McKinley High School, which was outside my neighbourhood and would require special approval. McKinley was renowned as the public high school with the best record in Washington DC for its students being accepted into university, outside the prestigious private schools scattered across the suburbs. It was a predominantly black school, but in a more middle-class neighbourhood (akin to Decile 7), reinforcing the potency of socioeconomic status when it comes to the quality of education.

I liked McKinley because of its strong focus on science, with some cool physics and chemistry labs, complete with white smocks for the students to wear. We were encouraged to put our names on the smocks, so several of my friends and I had our names stitched on as 'Dr'. It was fun to look in the mirror and see 'Dr Hillman' staring back at me. I wanted to make my father proud of his son for one day bringing that dream to life. I had no idea about a process to think through which universities I might apply to, but I figured it would all sort itself out by the time I reached my senior year, which is when you applied for college entry. There were the preliminary scholastic aptitude tests that high school seniors took during their first semester, which then had direct impact on which schools you would apply to. My aptitude test scores were average at best. I had never taken an exam like that before and felt a bit overwhelmed by the experience, not knowing that many white students who lived in the suburbs took four-week tutorials to prepare for the same exam, paid for by their parents. That was not an option available to me, but I was learning as I went through the process. I was optimistic that I would attend university.

And so, it happened. I applied to four schools and was accepted by two, both outside DC, both offering full scholarships. I considered myself to be in the 'freshman class' of affirmative action in the early 1970s, when universities and businesses started targeting racial and ethnic minorities, as well as women, to bring a more diverse face to education and business. Unfortunately, the notion of targets and

To put the culture shock into proper perspective, until that very day when I walked onto campus, I had never been in a conversation with a white kid.

quotas had negative backlash back then, especially in the absence of empirical data that would, three decades later, make a compelling business case for diversity. Back then, it felt like a numbers game. And I was one of five black students accepted by Muhlenberg College in 1973, a concerted effort by the school to diversify its student body. I was grateful for the opportunity and very excited about leaving home to live on a college campus in Allentown, Pennsylvania, a city that Billy Joel would make famous in a song only a few years later.

My life changed dramatically when my parents and siblings drove away after dropping me off at my dorm on Muhlenberg's campus. I had tears in my eyes as they departed, then I turned into a sea of white faces. This was indeed a very new experience for me, one that I hadn't fully anticipated until it started to unfold. To put the culture shock into proper perspective, until that very day when I walked onto campus, I had never been in a conversation with a white kid. Before Muhlenberg, I didn't know any white kids personally, not even one. At middle school and high school, I had a few white teachers, but they were adults, and the conversations were always focused on school stuff. Growing up in a predominantly black city, in a black family in a black neighbourhood, attending all-black schools, it never occurred to me how 'curious' it was to have lived the first 18 years of my life without ever once sitting down with a white kid to have a conversation. And there I was, a black kid now living in a predominantly white city, on a white campus in a very white neighbourhood, with kids my age all around me, some very curious about my experience of being a token.

I didn't know what the word 'token' meant until I went to Muhlenberg. It was there that I would gain some early insights about the ways in which diversity should and should not be done. Back then, it did feel like a numbers game to fill pre-determined quotas. Unfortunately, those quotas translated into the 'chosen few' being viewed by the majority as unqualified and taking away seats from qualified white students who, paradoxically, then considered themselves victims of discrimination. In fact, the expression 'reverse discrimination' is still commonly used in New Zealand to describe the intent of affirmative action. The implication is that you are fixing one wrong with another wrong, the undertone being that one group is gaining unfairly at the expense of another group's loss.

The prevalent mental model back in the early days of diversity and affirmative action was one that bred resentment, and certainly very little empathy for those who wore the token badge. Some of my first conversations with white students at Muhlenberg were about what it felt like to be 'one of five' as opposed to one of them. Even though the five black freshmen lived in different dorms, we always sat together in the cafeteria for lunch and dinner. Anthropologists would describe this as social kinship, where you huddle together with people like yourself for a sense of belonging, often to feel less exposed. This kinship often sparked the question from white students, 'Why do you guys always sit together?' Our reply to them was, 'Why do you guys always sit together?' At the time, we didn't think the irony in our reply landed with the impact we were hoping for. The word 'inclusion' had yet to work its way into the psyche of people who were still grappling with how to make the numbers game work.

> *The prevalent mental model back in the early days of diversity and affirmative action was one that bred resentment, and certainly very little empathy for those who wore the token badge.*

In my first semester at Muhlenberg, I really struggled, socially and academically, more so than ever before. As a fairly introverted and self-contained teenager, I hadn't anticipated what it would feel like to stand out for being different, especially when I preferred not to. I had the whole gay side of myself locked away in solitary confinement. However, my blackness was on full display, complete with a huge afro, bell bottoms and platform shoes. I looked like a dancer in the famous *Soul Train* line. One day, four guys from my dorm approached me to see if I would go along with a gag they wanted to play on one of our professors. They asked if they could blow cigarette smoke into my afro, then have me walk into the classroom with the smoke slowly emanating from the top of my head — like my hair was on fire. I went along with it because I wanted to fit in and belong, to be one of them. I was 19 years old then. I certainly don't think that I would let someone blow cigarette smoke into my hair today for their own amusement. Back then, though, I was happy to make the guys laugh. It felt good to be needed.

In high school, I had been an A student. However, at the end of my first semester at Muhlenberg, I earned three Cs and two Ds. Not a very impressive start at all. I struggled with some of the subjects like chemistry and algebra, the same ones that I had aced in high school. I found myself reluctant to speak out in class, often worried about whether I would sound smart enough, especially listening to how some of the white kids were so good at asserting a perspective with confidence, backed up by facts, stats and research. As that first semester progressed, I began to doubt whether I really knew how to study, certainly not in the same way that many of the white kids studied. It had not occurred to me before that there is a discipline around studying and preparing for exams. Many of the white students had private tutors while in high school, as well as having attended courses to help prepare for their college admissions exams. There was a substantive difference in the quality of education these white kids had been exposed to, compared to my experience growing up.

Given my modest grades, I began to question whether I was an actual token — the real deal, not as qualified as the white students, not able to compete on a level playing field. Still struggling to fit in and do well academically, I seriously pondered whether to drop out and leave Muhlenberg, especially given the requisite that I maintain a decent grade-point average to sustain the scholarship. After a conversation with my parents, I decided to give it another shot into the second semester to see what might change for the better on both the social and academic fronts. One thing was certain, I had to get some traction or else pack up my bags and move back home to DC, something I did not want to do.

There was a substantive difference in the quality of education these white kids had been exposed to, compared to my experience growing up.

The second semester started down the same path as the first, especially when the five fraternities on campus kicked off their 'rush' season, where they make a concerted effort to recruit freshmen from the dorms who, hopefully, will join their 'house' and build on the good (and not so good) traditions over the next three years. Being rushed by the fraternities was an annual ritual for freshmen who lived in the dorms, one I wasn't aware of until it became apparent that I was not on any of their invitation lists. Neither were the other two black male freshmen who lived in the other dorms. None of us were invited down to the fraternity houses for dinners or parties. All the white male freshmen were invited to one or more houses, but not the three of us. At a school where there were no black fraternities, we all still sat together in the cafeteria for our meals.

I could not appreciate the significance of that moment while in the moment, but the very short walk to ZBT that evening would have long-standing ramifications on the rest of my life.

And then one evening into the second semester, my world changed for the better. I was sitting in my dorm room, about to go to the cafeteria for dinner, when there was a knock at my door. I opened it to find three white freshmen standing there. They lived on the same floor as me in the dorm, just a few doors down. We were also in some of the same classes together. They were there to invite me to come with them to Zeta Beta Tau (ZBT), the Jewish fraternity on campus. They had spoken with some of the upperclassmen at ZBT about me. They told them that I was a good guy who they really liked. They added that none of the other fraternities had invited me down to their houses. The three freshmen asked if they could invite me to dinner. The upperclassmen said, 'Go to the dorm right now and bring Harold back with you.' And there they stood when I answered their knock at my door. I could not appreciate the significance of that moment while in the moment, but the very short walk to ZBT that evening would have long-standing ramifications on the rest of my life.

I didn't know anything about empathy at the time, but I constantly think back to how those three freshmen showed the deepest form of empathy on my behalf that evening. By inviting me into their fold and going out of their way to do something positive for me, even if for just one dinner, it truly gave me a first-hand experience of what it feels like to be wanted. And what it feels like to belong. When I walked into the fraternity with them that night, the upperclassmen walked over to greet me. They all shook my hand and welcomed me, inviting me to sit with the other freshmen to enjoy a steak dinner, prepared by the frat's own personal chef, named Ginz. Honestly, I felt like a plant soaking up buckets of water after a very long drought. The experience was not only nourishing to my appetite, but also to my spirit.

In a Jewish fraternity, on a white Lutheran campus, I learned what it feels like to belong. As a religious minority in America and across the world, those young Jewish students could understand what it is like to be judged on the basis of their heritage or how they choose to worship, rather than their merit. They knew from their own personal experiences how stereotypes can often sting. Not only could they understand what it is like to NOT be invited for dinner, they could also relate to what it feels like to be overlooked or rejected, because you are different. Before university and prior to meeting the guys at ZBT, I knew very little about the Holocaust and the historical oppression of Jews. There is something very connecting when you have walked in the shoes of another person. Those three freshmen had likely worn those same shoes before, to know what it feels like to be excluded. They went the extra step to get me invited to dinner. It was a tangible act of compassion, one that meant the world to me, both at the time and still today. I was so happy to be welcomed as a guest.

Long story short, ZBT invited me to pledge their fraternity that semester, which I proudly did. I was the first black guy to join a fraternity at Muhlenberg College and was a rare gem in the annals of ZBT's national heritage at the time. In the hallways of our fraternity house, there were group photos of each class dating back over the previous 20 years. My face stood out as unique in our fraternity photos, something I cherished with pride rather than angst. For the first time since walking onto campus months earlier, I felt a real sense of home and what it meant to belong. I moved down to the fraternity house in my second year, when I really started to thrive. Belonging to a family of loving brothers made a huge difference for me. I was eventually elected President of the fraternity in my senior year.

> *I can personally attest to the impact a sense of belonging has on confidence and performance.*

I can personally attest to the impact a sense of belonging has on confidence and performance. In that dismal first semester, I couldn't seem to get traction, undoubtedly fuelled by not knowing whether or where I fit in or belonged. My confidence eroded quickly, my grades suffered and I seriously debated whether to drop out. Thankfully, the second semester was a shining contrast. After joining ZBT, I earned three Bs and two As, an average I would sustain across the next three years, strong enough to propel me into Harvard University for a master's degree, then on to the University of Pittsburgh for my doctorate in clinical psychology.

Am I suggesting that a simple dinner invitation from a college fraternity changed the entire trajectory of my life? I most certainly am. Compassionate empathy comes in many forms, but the impact is one that resonates deeply whenever it touches you. A small gesture can make a big difference in the lives of many people who simply want to fit in, belong and be their best. Is there someone in your personal or professional life who would appreciate an invitation to dinner? Takeaway is fine. Remember, it's the intent that matters.

COMPASSIONATE EMPATHY
KEY THEMES FROM THE CASE STORIES

1. The Golden Rule

Mark could sense Andy was doubting his own confidence at the table, being the new guy who now felt like a deer in headlights on the team. He could relate based on his own experience two years earlier when he would have appreciated someone taking him aside for a supportive chat.

Theo's story exemplifies why leadership should not be defined by rank, but rather by the courage to bring your voice when it matters most. By taking a stand for Sandra, he risked alienating his older mates, but he went there anyway. The impact was powerful from the youngest member of the team, who taught the oldest members something about respect.

'Do unto others as you would have them do unto you.' I could feel that very sentiment from the three white freshmen in my dorm who took it upon themselves to get me an invitation to dinner, then personally escorted me to the fraternity as their friend. We are all still in touch today.

2. The Extra Mile

There is something wired deep in a person's character when they act on your behalf to make a real difference. Theo acted on Sandra's behalf, going the extra mile, exercising discretion so as not to upset her. Mark debated the same around how he could support Andy without the unintended consequence of making him feel inadequate — how to intervene with someone who is having an issue with confidence, while not exacerbating the very issue.

My experience with ZBT was much larger than delicious meals, although the Thursday night steak dinners were always the highlight of the week. Two of the senior upperclassmen took a real liking to me and coached me on study techniques I had never learned before, such as index cards, yellow marker highlighters and thematic analysis. That was the first time I had ever been coached by someone my own age. It was an awesome experience, especially knowing they were coming from a good place in their heart, going the extra mile to help their new black brother succeed.

3. Just Plain Awesome

People who are intrinsically motivated are deeply connected to values and principles that shape how they live. Mark, Theo and my three friends at Muhlenberg all reflected something about where their values were rooted, each wanting to make a real positive difference for another person. And the impact from each was just plain awesome. You know that feeling when someone goes out of their way to make a difference in your life. Be awesome to someone today.

Conversation Boosters

Here are some ways to navigate your way into or through a conversation where compassionate empathy can make a big difference.

Compassionate Empathy Mindset

- Compassion is a feeling of deep sympathy and sorrow for another person who is stricken by misfortune, accompanied by a desire to help alleviate their pain and suffering.
- Empathy is best conveyed when you are fully present, there in the moment with another person. You make space for them with no distractions.
- While compassion may entail some expense in effort, time or even capital, the gift is secondary to knowing that you have made a real difference for someone in need.
- Sometimes it may be important for people to know that you support a particular cause, when they learn why you have contributed your time and effort and how you want to make a difference.
- Anonymity also works, especially if the person can benefit from a surge of empowerment, taking pride in how they worked their way through a particular situation.

What Not to Say

Everything happens for a reason. You'll see that one day.

You'll get over it soon enough. It's a process you have to go through.

Surprise! We know how much you miss Rover, so we bought you a new puppy.

You can try for another baby again soon.

I'll figure this all out and come back with a solution for you.

Let me save you some time here and cut to the chase.

What to Say

How can I be most helpful to you?

I understand and feel where you are right now. I've been there before myself.

Is there any particular perspective that I can lend to you over the next little while, which may help you to land in a good place?

Here is what worked for me in a similar scenario. Modify it to what works best for you.

To and from the chain of command: Make this situation right. It goes against who we are. And then let's discuss what we learned.

On social media: Here is why I am taking a stand.

Anonymously: Hope this makes your day.

Landing with Impact

I know what you are going through and want to be helpful, but I don't want to overstep my boundaries. How can I best support you right now?

I know how important personal pride is to you, same as for me. For both of us, it is easier to give than to receive. But every now and then, it is okay to receive. This may be one of those times.

We care about you, for so many reasons, but mostly for how much you have helped us all succeed. You have always given so much of yourself. This is our way to say thanks and to support you.

How about I just come over and hang out with you, bring along some music, we can sing some tunes, have a few good laughs?

On a COVID-19 hospital unit: Your family cannot be here with you. I will hold your hand and pray with you. I promise to be at your side if you pass away.

11

BUILDING YOUR EMPATHY TOOLKIT: THE THREE CIRCLES

An Energy Exchange. Connection is all about the flow and exchange of energy between two or more people. The energy that enables or disables connection resides within each of us and moves between three zones, best described as circles, on a continual basis. The circles are neither good nor bad, only human. You toggle between them, sometimes consciously, but many times you are not even aware when you have crossed from one circle into another.

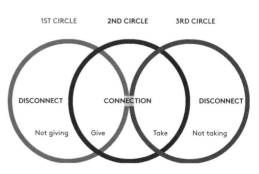

Think of the circles as individual zones you inhabit and often co-habit with others. People who have strong self-awareness are more purposeful about which circle they are in, while those who lack it are often caught by surprise when a conversation starts to unravel badly. To build self-awareness, you have to know the three circles and the impact of each on your ability to lead with influence.

Your energy flows into First Circle when you choose to, or unknowingly, go inward. Someone observing you in First Circle will notice that you have become quieter, maybe even a bit withdrawn. People will experience you as pensive or distracted, perhaps deliberating something deep in your own mind. Sometimes in First Circle you may be in the room with other people, but not really there *with* them. Even in a one-on-one conversation with someone, you may not be there. You are not present. Your head is somewhere else. Because your energy is drawn inward, the other person feels little to no connection. You are not giving them anything to grab hold of.

Third Circle is at the other end of the energy flow. It is the opposite of First Circle energy. Rather than withdrawing inward and becoming insular, your energy flows outward, very often in surges that can feel aggressive or intimidating, especially if you are the boss. In a one-on-one conversation, a person in Third Circle is usually doing all the talking and directing. Under pressure, you may even come across as rigid and defensive. Limited self-awareness only accelerates the disconnect that inevitably happens. When you are in Third Circle, the impact is the same as when in First Circle. You are there in the room, but not really present. In full force Third Circle, you are unwilling to receive anything offered. After a while, the person stops giving. With you not taking, connection is broken.

Fight or Flight. Like most people, you have loads of experience in life toggling between the two ends of the energy continuum. As humans, we are wired to ward off any potential threat to our sense of stability or safety, whether that threat be another person, a natural disaster, even a global pandemic. Under perceived threat, anxiety is a natural physical and mental response to your body's sudden surge of adrenaline (to fuel you) and cortisol (to focus you). When this happens, you are instinctively wired to either flee the threat or attack it. Most people know this very human reaction as the *fight or flight* response. At some level, the chances are high that you have experienced one or the other within the past week.

Flight is about quickly directing your energy into First Circle, where you make yourself as small a target as possible. You can see it in the person's posture, even hear it in their voice, like they are retreating inward. Have you ever tried to make yourself invisible at a meeting where you didn't feel safe? Then there's *fight*, akin to the energy that happens when you dive into Third Circle. In fight mode, like a blowfish under attack, you make yourself as big as possible to ward off a perceived threat. Have you ever locked down on a particular issue, like a dog with a bone who won't let it go? Same as with First Circle, most people can relate to occasionally going into Third. Under any perceived threat, you will either pull your energy inward or force it aggressively outward. In First Circle, you aren't giving anything. In Third Circle, you aren't taking anything. When neither person is willing to give or take anything from the other, the relationship is broken. This is why many personal and professional relationships falter.

Impostor Syndrome. If you have ever experienced impostor syndrome, you will know what a broken connection feels like. People who feel like impostors spend a lot of their time in either First or Third circle, often switching feverishly between the two. When you wear the impostor's mask, you fear being exposed as imperfect, all the while missing the point that imperfection actually enables connection. In contrast, the need to be perfect disables connection because you are less likely to ask for support. Connection is born when two or more people need each other for what each has to offer. It is broken when everyone reaches for their mask to be the perfect person. All the more reason to know when you are likely to go into either First or Third circle and how to minimise your time there.

First Circle Scenarios	**Third Circle Scenarios**
• Newest or least experienced person on the team; reluctant to give	• Oldest or most experienced person on the team; can't lose respect
• Exiting the team soon and wondering if your views still matter to others	• Hired from the outside when there were internal candidates
• Limited knowledge on a topic; not wanting to expose yourself	• Considered the expert on a topic; not wanting to expose yourself
• In an interim role, not backing yourself to bring your voice	• Under certain pressures of which others are unaware
• On a dysfunctional team, where putting yourself out there is risky	• On a dysfunctional team, where retreating inward is risky

The Power of Second Circle. Notice that the three circles are not distinct entities sitting side by side with clear boundaries between them. The three circles overlap to create a wonderful confluence point between the two outer circles. This point of confluence is in Second Circle. It contains the optimal zones of both First and Third circles, where you are reflective without detaching, persuasive without dominating. When two or more people are in Second Circle together, the connection they feel is palpable. It is analogous to breathing, a natural and rhythmic cadence between inhaling (taking in) and exhaling (giving out). There is an unmistakeably positive exchange of energy going on.

In Second Circle, you don't feel the need to be perfect, which then negates that sense of feeling exposed. You are not worried about having to protect your status or ego by being the one who wins. There is no contest in play. It is about putting *our* best thinking on the table, willing to listen to each other to learn rather than to find fault. The goal is not about one person winning and the other losing, but winning together. Success is about getting the best outcome, not about preserving your infallibility. You are really comfortable with who you are — and who you aren't. This helps to put the people around you at ease; it makes it easier for them to come into Second Circle with you.

A talented friend, who plays in a jazz quartet, believes they perform best when all are in Second Circle together. The connection is partly intuitive, hard to put into words, but definitely grounded in a strong sense of trust where they are willing to follow someone's lead and everyone then synchronises, perhaps in a different way from the previous night's performance. When watching a quartet on stage, you are drawn into their spontaneity and fluidity with one another. They are following each other's lead, knowing when to bring it and when to make room for someone else to do so. In Second Circle together, there is a give and take on stage, which creates a connection you can feel from the audience. During live performances, stage directors keep their eyes on the audience to determine whether their connection is palpable with the

There is no contest in play. It is about putting our best thinking on the table, willing to listen to each other to learn rather than to find fault.

performers on stage. A broken connection with the audience means a broken connection on the stage. You can see the clear parallels to business. If the top team are rarely in Second Circle together, that same dynamic will play out across the wider organisation.

Empathy and Circles. It helps to think of empathy as an energy exchange, a give and take between two or more people. It is literally that feeling of relief when someone finally understands where you are coming from, or why you feel the way you do. When deep in First or Third Circle, you make little effort to understand another person's point of view. You are either not interested or too busy defending your own stance. By increasing your time in Second Circle, people will experience you as more curious and eager to learn, where you genuinely convey what you have taken in, even if you decide not to support the idea. There is a genuineness about you when in Second Circle with another person or the team, reinforcing the correlation between being yourself and allowing others to do the same. That is the zone when the real magic happens. To be an effective leader, be more mindful about which circle you are in.

12

BUILDING YOUR EMPATHY TOOLKIT: TO BE PRESENT

It runs deep. Analogous to the proverbial iceberg, presence is a massive entity that has a huge impact on how you experience life. It is both tall and wide, the snow-capped tip most apparent to the eye, with the bulk of its essence immersed deep in the water and out of sight. When it comes to presence, people are naturally drawn to what they see above the water line — the more compelling aesthetics such as beauty, intellect, confidence and inspiration. Yes, presence is about looking good, sounding strong and delivering an uplifting message. Image consultants stress the importance of these surface aesthetics on your ability to influence successful outcomes. But we also know the aesthetics are wired into the deeper regions of a person's psychology, down to the very base of the iceberg where thoughts, beliefs and values reside. You won't find self-awareness at the tip of the iceberg. To learn more about yourself, you have to put on the snorkel and dive deep around your own thinking.

For example, it is difficult to convey empathy when you are absorbed with being the winner in a scenario where collaboration would get a better outcome. The fix here is not about saying the right words to make people believe that their views really matter. 'I value your opinion' sounds good on the surface, certainly enough to draw people in. To keep them with you requires something more fundamental than any clever catchphrase. Your choice of words is important, but they will have little impact if your aching desire is to be the most dominant person at the table. People know it when you are not really interested in what they have to say. They see your thoughts and beliefs manifested through your actions, even when you can't. Yet another reason why it helps to be self-aware in a leadership role.

The Four Dimensions of Presence. Four dimensions define what it means to be fully present with another person, or even with an audience of hundreds.

- The first dimension is about being here, in the moment, now.
- The second dimension entails you making more space to absorb experiences devoid of clutter.
- The third dimension requires you to suspend judgements that might otherwise block empathy.
- The fourth dimension is about genuine connection shown through respect.

DIMENSION 1: HERE AND NOW

In the Moment. You may be sitting in a café or walking through a park. You might be on a ferry on your way to work. Or alone in a room listening to music. Tune into the sensations around and within you. During the first COVID lockdown, a client was working from her home office, which overlooked the back yard. The window was open and she heard two birds talking to each other in the most beautiful chirps. She was drawn in to their conversation, especially their rhythmic cadence back and forth. The birds were definitely talking to each other. She looked out to see them on two branches, one slightly above the other. They were facing each other and hopping about. Their tone was playful. She was captivated. It was a moment she had not experienced in a very long time. She could not believe how beautiful the sounds and colours were in that tree. That is when she realised how much time she spends with her head down. There are so many sensations happening all around you. Practise spending more time in the moment.

The Present Tense. It is difficult to be fully present when your energy is focused on something that happened last week or on something that may happen in two days. In a meeting, pay close attention to your thoughts about the person who is speaking. Is your lens on that person's perspective clouded by a conversation you had with them last week, maybe some emotion that triggers you to either lean in or push away? To be fully present with someone requires you to be in the present tense together. You are here with them, not over there, not stuck in the past, not obsessed with the future. Your ability to live in the moment is such a huge part of being present. Learn to really be with someone, really there, same as in Second Circle. Present tense.

It might be time to confront the popular notion that multitasking is a skill that we want to build muscle around.

DIMENSION 2: MAKE SPACE

Declutter Your Mind. Some people wear their ability to multitask as a badge of honour. Mothers are often credited with an innate gift to juggle competing needs on the work and home fronts, yet somehow make it happen with almost flawless resilience. It might be time to confront the popular notion that multitasking is a skill that we want to build muscle around. On the surface, the ability to allocate your energy and focus simultaneously across multiple tasks seems like a great way to get a lot done at once. But research has shown that our brains are not nearly as good at handling multiple tasks as we like to think they are. In fact, some researchers point out that multitasking can actually reduce productivity by as much as 40 per cent, particularly when the person is under pressure and fatigue sets in.

Several studies have shown that high multitaskers experience greater problems focusing on important and complicated tasks, memory impairment of new subject matter, difficulty learning new material and increased stress levels. These indicators shout out loudly that you should make more space in your psyche for fewer priorities. The rule of three might prevail here too. Should you make it a priority to declutter your mind over the next month, or even longer? In any given day across any given week, would you be better served to focus your energy on those things that matter the most, whether in your personal or work space? Give it a go and see if it makes a difference to your ability to focus and channel your energy for maximum impact. Your empathy is more palpable when you are fully present. Make more space for your psyche to breathe.

Minimise Interruptions. The COVID-19 pandemic certainly highlighted the many positives associated with working virtually, especially the ability to minimise countless interruptions that impede your ability to focus on something important for more than just a few minutes before the next ding of your mobile phone. At your typical on-site work location in open space, chalk up roughly two hours each day of lost time trying to refocus after an average of 56 interruptions each day. Across a given week, you lose roughly one day of productivity in the grand experiment of open space.

The constant onslaught of emails also factors into lost productivity. Here are some stark facts from Atlassian that show how technology, once deemed the great enabler for communication, may actually make it harder to focus while at work. On average, you receive 304 business-related emails each week. You are likely to check your email 36 times every hour while at work. And it takes about 16 minutes to get refocused after replying to two incoming emails. Across a given day, that amounts to roughly two hours where your focus is diluted. Have you been distracted by an email since you started reading this chapter? Chances are high the answer is 'yes'.

Some businesses are now challenging the prevalent mindset that a meeting should run for 60 minutes, a practice that is rooted in the industrial era dating back to the previous century.

Pace Your Energy. Along with the constant interruptions and bombardment of emails, there are also the endless meetings where you spend most of your time across a given day. As with emails and interruptions, you have little control over making meetings disappear. They are an essential fact of life; a way for people to make meaning together around an important topic before they disperse to take action. The problem is, the protocol around meetings is sloppy and loose in many organisations, which is a major cause of frustration for busy people who have very little time to waste. Some businesses are now challenging the prevalent mindset that a meeting should run for 60 minutes, a practice that is rooted in the industrial era dating back to the previous century. In this modern information age, we do not require as much time to sit together in the same room to make decisions. We learned this during the first COVID lockdown when many people and teams reported greater productivity and efficiency associated with shorter meetings.

Pre-COVID, Atlassian reported that, on average, most employees attend 65 meetings each week. Half of these meetings are considered time wasted, with roughly 33 hours every month deemed unproductive. Up to 91 per cent of us daydream in meetings, while 39 per cent occasionally doze off into a real nap. Further, 73 per cent do other work in meetings, while 45 per cent feel overwhelmed by the number of meetings they attend and 47 per cent believe that meetings are the number one waste of time in their day. The negative impact from the same research is compelling. Salary costs for unnecessary meetings in

US businesses alone is $37 billion. In more ways than one, there is definitely a price tag attached to wasted time. Are there ways for you to be more productive and present at work? Take a look at your weekly diary to see if you can make space to be more present with people in the moment. It is difficult to convey empathy if people experience you as a blur — constantly dashing to the next meeting.

DIMENSION 3: SUSPEND JUDGEMENT

Mindfulness. Mindfulness has gained more resonance in the business world over the past decade. For many people, the catalyst has been a very personal experience with a drop in productivity and engagement when they don't make enough space in their lives to be fully present. Presence is tantamount to mindfulness. Many people see them as one and the same.

In its simplest and purest domain, you are mindful when conscious and accepting of the present moment, without feeling the need to pass judgement. Mindfulness is a constant awareness of your thoughts, emotions and sensations, and how they affect your state of being as well as others around you. It involves looking at a situation, accepting whatever is happening and having the clarity of mind to face the situation productively. When mindful, you are largely in an observer's role, to learn rather than to evaluate. This is about your ability to suspend judgement, which is easier said than done.

A practical example. Jim is in a meeting where he is trying to practise being mindful. He is fascinated by this notion of being an observer, in real time, to his own thoughts and feelings. For the past 15 minutes, Jim has observed himself detach off and on from the budget discussion. Some things pull him in, but he is mostly detached, especially when the focus is on someone else's division. Jim becomes aware of a prevalent thought driving his detachment: 'This has nothing to do with me.' He can feel his energy drop when he surmises there is nothing he can contribute to the conversation. Even if he thought to ask something, he would probably hesitate. 'That would feel intrusive if it happened to me,' he tells himself. Jim now wonders if everyone has the same goal — to get through their bit as quickly as possible, without any questions. When it comes to budget discussions, there is an implicit ethic on this team: 'If you don't question me, I won't question you.' Jim wonders if it is time for the team to re-frame the purpose of these discussions. *What can we learn from each other? What can we give to each other?* Those two questions cause him to focus with more interest for the rest of the discussion. Jim is eager to test a theory born from his own observation. Should he change his position on the role he can play in these budget discussions? He reckons it is a theory worth testing. This is what mindfulness looks like in action.

Curiosity. When it comes to being present, curiosity is definitely a positive energy force. A compelling example of the power of curiosity is that of Daryl Davis, who delivered a TED Talk in 2018 entitled, 'Klan We Talk?' Davis is a black musician who befriended Robert Kelly, who was then an Imperial Wizard of the Ku Klux Klan, infamous for its legacy of white supremacy and hatred toward black people in America. They met following a performance by Davis's band at a night club, where Kelly introduced himself and told Davis that he had never seen a black guy play 'country music' before. They continued to chat over the next few months in that same club, growing a friendship that would be life changing for both.

Kelly was struck by how Davis neither judged nor rejected him because of his KKK affiliation. And Davis was struck by Kelly's bond with him, for the same reason, best described as not feeling judged.

Kelly was struck by how Davis neither judged nor rejected him because of his KKK affiliation. And Davis was struck by Kelly's bond with him, for the same reason, best described as not feeling judged. Eventually, Kelly invited Davis to his home and then to Klan rallies in which ritualistic chants were intoned, giant crosses were burned, and beer and hot dogs were served. To imagine a black guy at a KKK rally conjures up the worst images of humanity. Yet, these two guys made it happen as they built a friendship. Kelly shared everything with Davis, including the deep racial stereotypes that helped to form the foundation of the Klan's hatred. All the while, Davis listened to Kelly, asked questions, took notes and, through his actions, slowly dispelled each stereotype one by one. With each conversation, the gap between them narrowed and they were able to become friends.

As a result of their bond, Kelly quit the Klan, shut down his entire chapter and, as a trophy of sorts, gave his robe to Davis. That was not the last Ku Klux Klan robe that Davis would be gifted, nor was it the last Klansman he would befriend. In total, nearly 200 Klansmen quit the KKK as a result of Davis's curiosity to understand who they were as people, not as villains. His empathy toward them helped to melt their negative stereotypes about black people. This is a perfect example of how curiosity can open up the energy between people who might otherwise focus on their differences.

DIMENSION 4: SHOW RESPECT

Good Manners. The fourth dimension of presence is mostly about being a decent person. We associate decency with someone whose values reflect a strong regard for respect and civility. A respectful person makes room for the needs of others and is more purposeful about what may be important to a person in their space, especially around their quality of life. For example, your Muslim colleague makes time to pray five times daily — at dawn, midday, afternoon, sunset and then at night before going to bed. When he is at work, you respect his need to pull away for a few minutes to practise his faith, without judgement or reservation. Your respect allows him the space to do so, even adjusting the meeting start times to accommodate for something that is fundamentally important to him and not a big deal on your part to be flexible. Respect is about taking the time to know what really matters to another person and signifying that through your behaviour.

Respect is about taking the time to know what really matters to another person and signifying that through your behaviour.

Civility walks hand in hand with respect. The best way to describe civility is to highlight someone with proper manners. Your mother's advice to 'mind your manners' is not only important to whether people like you and prefer to be around you, but it is also critical to business success. Manners go a long way in business. People like to be treated with civility. Your ability to build rapport is the first crucial step in building strong relationships, networking and closing sales. When business leaders are surveyed on what they consider to be examples of professionalism, 'good manners' ranks among the top answers. This should be no surprise to anyone who has walked away from doing business with a person who lacked civility or proper interpersonal savvy. Can you think of someone you distanced yourself from because their behaviour ran counter to your values? There is a price to pay for being a crass person.

Collaboration. This word is used a lot in business. Many companies list 'collaboration' as one of their core values, to exemplify how they expect people to work together. Like many company values, it can be taken for granted as a given, versus something that you have to work at. Collaboration is deeper than just doing business together. Perhaps the best description comes in a TED Talk by Ken Blanchard, where he describes the change in mindset he made early in his career to write over 60 books, most of which were co-authored. Blanchard highlights how status, ego and pride are huge impediments to collaboration. If you have to win in every conversation, you will struggle to be fully present. Presence requires a 'give and take' when collaborating, where there is no winner or loser. You simply want the best thinking to prevail. Sounds a lot like being in Second Circle.

13

BUILDING YOUR EMPATHY TOOLKIT: ACTIVE LISTENING

Oops. Have you ever walked away from a conversation wondering how it could have turned out so badly? You started with the best of intentions. To listen. And then everything seemed to unravel. Worse still, you learn later you have a reputation as a poor listener. More than just a handful of spouses in the world have had that label thrown at them on occasion.

Listening is a gift many people don't realise they possess, a gift that would make such a difference to so many others who sometimes simply need to be heard. Or validated. Or understood and appreciated. Or told they are not going crazy. With the best of intentions, people who think they are listening in a supportive way often find out, the hard way, that their efforts to help have backfired. There is such a thing as listening in a bad way. Like cutting the person off, or shaking your head in disdain, or sighing loudly, or continuing to text while they talk, or telling them why they shouldn't think a certain way, or feel a certain way, or evaluating their judgement in a very judgemental way. It is difficult for someone to feel empathy when any of this is going on.

Many people treat listening as a passive thing rather than an active way to build trust and rapport. Sitting across from someone while they talk does not constitute listening. To hear is one thing — an auditory sensation. To listen to someone moves beyond the ear's wiring. Listening is more of an active choice to plug into a conversation. Still, even with the intent to listen well, some people are much better at it than others. It is an acquired skill that correlates strongly with emotional intelligence. To listen deeply to another person is the most significant way to convey empathy. We know that people who feel listened to are more engaged and take more ownership for outcomes. You can easily make a business case for why *learning to listen well* should not be left to chance. Arguably, it has direct impact on your bottom line.

How Do You Want Me to Listen? This is not a rhetorical question. It is a way you can start a conversation with someone who has requested your ear for any number of reasons. My experience has taught me there are six ways to listen to another person, hence the need for leaders to become more adept at a skill that can make or break how you engage with people. A big part of growing adept at listening is learning to trust your intuition more, which often requires you to see with your ears and hear with your eyes. There is also a more basic way to know which listening mode you need to be in when a person requests a few minutes of your time to work through something important. Ask them how they would like you to listen. A good listener is mindful of what others may need in the moment, so why not get on the same frequency from the onset? Share the ownership for a successful outcome to the conversation. 'For me to be of most help, *how would you like me to listen?*'

1. Listen as a Valve.

This listening style is the most difficult for leaders because it requires that you be in the moment with the person, able to suspend an opinion or resist trying to fix anything, instead allowing that person to be emotive about something that has hit a button or sore spot. We have all been there. Just like a radiator full of compressed air, a person sometimes needs the space to blow off some steam. As the listener on the other end of this exchange, sometimes the best thing you can do is just let it happen.

If you are inclined to grow impatient when people are having one of those moments, you should explore the message this sends around your tolerance for them to have an emotive connection with their work. Allow people around you to be human when they need to blow off some steam, perhaps even to hear themselves say out loud what they have been struggling with for a while. Giving a person or team the space to decompress is often followed by them acknowledging that 'staying stuck' is not an option. Through your willingness to hear them, they can begin to build their own action plan to move beyond the current pain. Your challenge is to suspend judgement, provide space and shut up (but not shut out) long enough for this to happen.

> Try listening as a valve when…
> - someone interprets a change in direction as a personal defeat
> - those remaining after a staff reduction feel a sense of loss or guilt
> - results are disappointing in spite of tremendous effort
> - you have redefined roles and responsibilities and someone feels demoted
> - you sense someone needs the space to talk about something difficult
> - results are good, but everybody is tired and wondering what's coming next.

2. Listen to Reflect.

The skill and value here is in your ability to serve as a mirror, as a way to help the person gain clarity and meaning. You are reflecting the speaker's experience back to them, an effort to impose some meaning and interpretation on their perspective. Reflection often brings meaning to emotion. But, as the listener in this mode, you must distance yourself from the speaker's emotion. The meaning is what the speaker imposes, not you. Your role is to reflect back their words so they can listen for the meaning in them.

Listening to reflect can be a challenge, especially if you sense the person is too hard, or in some cases, too easy on themselves. You may want to offer support or impose judgement, but this may not be what is needed in the moment. Offering support or imposing judgement in the absence of meaning can be futile and frustrating for the person. When listening to reflect, you help to create meaning and context that will often spark something for them.

As a mirror, you have to detach from your own views. Let your eyes and ears become your primary source for reflection. As little of you as possible should be reflected in what the speaker hears. You have become a conduit for their voice and experience to flow directly to their ears. A conduit channels energy. It can also channel meaning. Often, in the absence of meaning, you can listen to the speaker with greater clarity. Be the mirror. Help to bring clarity.

Try listening to reflect when…
- someone is closing in on a strategy and needs to hear how their own logic is building
- you believe the person's thinking is cluttered and they may benefit from hearing it played back to them in smaller bites
- someone is moving way too fast and has not made the time to stop and take stock of what's happening
- someone seems surprised or confused about why others react to them in a certain way
- as the listener, you are confused and need to slow the person down to probe for meaning.

3. Listen for Assumptions.

This style will require some diligent focus on your part, so be sure to minimise distractions when you go there. Listening for assumptions requires you to be on top of every word. The speaker invites you to signal any flawed aspects of reasoning that may be based on faulty assumptions. We all carry around theories in our heads about why people do what they do, why things work the way they work, why we get the results we get. Any theory can push you, subliminally, toward action quicker than you would like to consider. In fact, many of your theories are untested because they make perfect sense to you. This is called unconscious bias — things you can't see in yourself, but others can see reflected in your decisions. When someone asks you to listen for assumptions in their thinking, you can help them to understand the link between their theories and choices.

In a typical business, you will hear loads of assumptions made about what key stakeholders need and will accept. Listen carefully for where others may be taking for granted the perspective of customers, employees, contractors in your supply chain, even the shareholders. If someone appears to breeze by in their logic about a key stakeholder group, this may be a sign that their lenses are too comfortable. Lift their spectacles, blur their vision a bit and then make them more conscious about how precarious a certain assumption may be. By probing for data that supports or refutes a theory about the way a person works, you help them update their spectacles to remain current with change.

Try listening for assumptions when…
- you hear little evidence of data that support major conclusions
- someone continues to box themselves in and is reluctant to push at perceived boundaries
- someone continues to rush by, over, and through perceived boundaries
- innovative thinking is missing
- you believe that the speaker's rank or seniority is prohibiting others from probing deeply around their assumptions.

4. Listen as the Contrarian.

The term 'contrarian' says it all about the person who wears this title. We all know the concept. This is someone who finds the holes in your position and then advocates the opposite, or a noticeably different viewpoint. This is the person who comes across as contrary. Some of these people are contrary by nature, all day long, forever and ever. Let's take a little slice of that oppositional nature and define it as a listening style that, when done well, opens up the opportunity to discover holes or deficiencies in someone's thinking. It is a technique often taught in formal debate. Your role is to listen as the contrarian, the one who pushes back, sometimes hard, from the opposing side.

Listening as the contrarian enables you to table issues that are often difficult to raise otherwise. Whether one on one or in team meetings, there are defensive routines that play out to the point where you dance around the important issues. Often, people are reluctant to point out where they see holes in logic or raise legitimate concerns out of fear that they will embarrass or humiliate either themselves or the speaker. Consequently, the learning and, possibly, the decision suffers because these defensive routines prevail.

Try listening as the contrarian when…
- you believe others are too polite to say what they really feel
- you believe others are too political to say what they really feel
- you get the impression the team is coming to consensus on a decision too quickly
- there is not enough diversity of perspective on the team
- there are just too many gaping holes in the logic.

5. Listen for Balance.

Some people see the world through a lens of what is possible. Other people see that same world through a different lens that focuses on what is probable. Like most things in life, too much of either is a bad thing. Predictably, a healthy blend of both works best.

People who think in terms of what is possible prefer to broaden the scope of their thinking. They are divergent thinkers who get energy from focusing on the big picture. There is clearly an upside to this vantage, but as is the case with many polarities, there is also a potential downside. Along with the *big picture* may come the tendency to overlook important details and facts that are germane to the story. As the listener, you can help to infuse essential details that help anchor the bigger picture to some tangible practicalities.

Then there are the people who prefer to converge in their thinking, focused on narrowing down their options supported by loads of empirical data. These people like to think in terms of what is probable and will use deductive reasoning to land on a certain position. If someone who thinks this way invites you to listen to their ideas, you can help by elevating the conversation above the data to focus more on where the conversation needs to go. Another way to think about your role is that of inflating the idea, much like you would inflate a balloon. You stretch the walls, which creates, in many cases, a different shape.

You can appreciate how important it is to infuse this listening style if everyone on the team thinks in one particular way. Sometimes you may have to go out of your comfort zone to infuse the other perspective, just to make sure there is enough balance in the thinking.

> Try listening for balance when…
> - you hear too much big picture and not enough detail
> - you hear too much detail and not enough big picture
> - the point in time of the strategy's evolution requires balance
> - the speaker seems locked in one particular view or broadly dismisses the other
> - you believe that it would be good, for your own development, to probe from the other side.

6. Listen for the System.

The premise behind this listening style is that no one can simultaneously observe and play. If you are a player, concede that you have a view and some biases. Most of the time, you have an opinion. This renders the pretence of objectivity about other players, and other plays, in the system false. The mental myopia in all of us limits the objectivity necessary to make the best decisions. We are often simply too close to it. It is a powerful gift if you can help reveal all aspects of the system that may be a part of either the problem or solution.

Systems theory tells us that every event we react to, and every event we anticipate, is connected to some deeper forces. These forces push on each other, like what happens under an iceberg. You often only realise what has happened after it surfaces on your radar screen. When you listen for the system, you broaden the thinking to consider ramifications well beyond your team's parameters. This way, you help to avoid any unanticipated consequences — by building in the opportunity to anticipate them.

> Try listening for the system when…
> - the scenario is complex and big, and requires many ears
> - you believe the team has come up with a superficial solution and needs to go deeper
> - there are multiple accountabilities that need to be ironed out before locking a plan in place
> - the plan requires different levels and layers of buy-in.

Lead with the Question. How do you want me to listen? And be willing and able to explain each style and the related benefits. Encourage the team to think about how they can influence the quality of conversation by requesting a listening style that leads to a better outcome. This is a shared accountability and everyone needs to understand the benefits of each style. This requires a conversation about conversation and, more specifically, about listening. Like most things intuitive, listening is truly an art.

14

BUILDING YOUR EMPATHY TOOLKIT: THE FIVE-POINT COACHING GAME PLAN

Your Coach Hat. Know the distinction between leading, managing, mentoring and coaching — four roles you can easily go between on any given day. Leading another person or team entails taking them toward a future they choose to buy into, often fuelled by your vision and inspiration. Managing a team requires you to be across the required protocols, processes and procedures that lead to the successful delivery of work — how we do things around here. Mentoring is sometimes very formal, and other times quite informal, where you pass along wisdom and perspective shaped by years of experience, hence the image of a wise, sage-like Yoda. And then there is coaching, which is a very effective way to demonstrate empathy, especially when you are helping to lift someone's capability or confidence.

You have the opportunity to wear your coach's hat many times a day, every day at work. And even when you are not at work, the impact of your coaching is still there. Here are a few examples to highlight when it is important to move into coaching mode:

- One of your direct reports is struggling to build the project plan for a major systems roll-out. A huge part of this person's struggle is having to put together the project plan, perhaps the biggest they have ever been asked to develop. But you also sense the person is having some self-doubts about their ability to lead the major roll-out. Your coaching could make a big difference in a scenario like this.
- A new team member is finding it difficult to build credibility in the organisation. Credibility goes to the heart of people trusting someone to deliver what they need, usually based on a track record. If people don't see the new team member as credible, they are unlikely to get on board, perhaps even work against the person's success. This is an ideal scenario where serving as a coach will enable the person to build a few strategies to help gain traction with critical stakeholders.
- There are times when you may choose to wear your coaching hat with a peer, say in the case of one who runs another division and is having difficulty landing a contract with a major customer. In this case, your peer may benefit from hearing what strategies have worked well for you when negotiating with a big customer or they can use you as a sounding board to test their own thinking and ideas about what might work.
- Or the challenge may be in coaching a team, say in the example of a team that has grown frustrated because they haven't made enough progress quickly on a critical project. Again, some of your coaching may be about a skill set that is missing among the team

members, but you will also want to keep close to the team's waning confidence. Your role as a coach may be to help the team regain its optimism and plan for ways to overcome obstacles in their path.

- Lastly, your coaching opportunity may be with your own manager, who may be a bit nervous about an upcoming presentation to the board. It is totally acceptable for a manager to learn from, and with, their direct reports. If you are a manager, you know how invigorating it is for a direct report to share their experience or perspective with you, especially if it leads to a successful outcome.

In these examples, and many others, you will get good at knowing when an opportunity presents itself for you to help another person, or the team, as a coach. These opportunities are all around you, every day, in many ways. A good coach recognises opportunities where they can make a difference. Where are your opportunities today to be a coach to someone who could use your support?

The Five-Point Coaching Game Plan. There are five key points to an effective coaching game plan.

1. Focus on the Prize

A prize is anything that is valued, worth striving for and, in some cases, seized. For any coaching goal, first, turn it into a prize, something that will motivate the person to push through any doubts or apprehension. Change the lens from that of the challenge being viewed as a problem, to one of opportunity. The energy derived from both lenses is vastly different. Optimism correlates strongly with mental and physical wellbeing, as well as successful leadership. Even when facing adversity, there are gains to be made. But do make sure that the size of the prize is in line with the person's (or the team's) capability to win it. When focusing on the prize, the goal should be attainable.

2. Prepare for the Stretch

In physics, there is an optimal zone for any object in stretch. On the stretch continuum, there are two extremes: *under-stretch* and *over-stretch*. *Optimal stretch* sits right in the middle. You can easily relate to times when you have either been very bored with a task, or emotionally daunted by its size. Not enough stretch can be as just as draining as too much stretch. Neither zone is optimal for performance. As a coach, you can help the person find the sweet spot around their required stretch, somewhere between those extremes. Capability and confidence are two things you want to keep your eye on. Are you asking the person to do something that is beyond their capability, which will likely have a negative impact on their confidence? The two Cs usually travel together. Be sure the energy around both is positive.

3. Reframe the Hurdles

Back to the notion of a goal as the prize, a person typically gains wisdom, even character, by facing obstacles and reframing them as hurdles, all part of succeeding in life. Your role as a coach is to help the person reframe the hurdles. As on a racing track, jumping over hurdles, they get stronger with every race. It is no different in business or in life. Encourage the person to plot the most direct path from the starting point to the prize. They should avoid workarounds that prevent dealing with hurdles as quickly as possible. Help them to determine what and where the major milestones are along the path. Then, for each milestone, have the person anticipate the major hurdles likely to impede progress. Help them to reframe those hurdles as opportunities. What skills will I learn from others along the way? What will I learn about myself, especially pushed outside my comfort zone? In a year's time, how will I be in a better position to influence successful outcomes?

4. Support with Straight Talk

Jack Welch, former Chair and CEO of General Electric, espoused that, as a leader, there is an ethic associated with being honest and candid with people. For Welch, straight talk was reflective of one's character, not to beat around the bush or deflect the conversation that needs to happen. In the interest of helping the person be successful, you have to be as candid as possible, always delivered with compassion. In fact, the compassion will be felt through your character. A person will know if you mean them well: *My goal in this conversation is not to hurt you, but to help you be successful.* Straight talk means bringing the good, bad and human into the conversation. It also requires timely discussions in relation to key milestones, rather than deferring them. The conversations, often guided by intuition and instinct, should be constructive and motivating. It is about knowing what is needed, and when. Straight talk — with candour, care and support.

5. Lock in the Learning

To help someone lock in a new way of doing something, or way of thinking, several things are important to consider as a coach. First, the person really should relish the prize, really celebrate the achievement. Some people want to immediately move to the next task without taking the time to relish the moment. Celebration is an important part of learning. It is also a healthy thing to do, often underplayed in New Zealand because of 'tall poppy syndrome'. When coaching, keep an eye out for whether the person has been able to stop and fully appreciate what has been accomplished. And to celebrate with the team as well. Then, be purposeful to reflect on all that has been learned and what adjustments might work better. It will also be important to reset development objectives or performance targets to ensure adequate stretch is built in for the person. Finally, encourage them to coach and teach others, which helps to build capability and confidence. To teach something to another person requires a heightened level of ownership and commitment.

15

BUILDING YOUR EMPATHY TOOLKIT: HOW PEOPLE THRIVE

Human Fulfilment. The beauty of leading people is they are not robots you can plug into an outlet at the beginning of the day and unplug as you are leaving. Yes, perhaps you have the occasional frustrating day when the option of robots sounds like a more ideal proposition, but real people bring colour and energy to any business challenge. Humans require a lot more work than robots, but the upsides are tangible. As a leader, it is important to understand the basic drivers of what is meaningful for most people in life, commonly referred to as human needs. Are you across what people need to grow and really thrive?

In the middle of the twentieth century, psychologist Abraham Maslow proposed his famous hierarchy of needs, which describes the pattern that drives human motivations from basic survival through to self-actualisation. Maslow's model is still pertinent and very relevant into a new century, which has already signalled to us that leadership and life will be different in a world with more unknown twists and turns. As a leader, it is important to know the basic components that lead to a sense of personal fulfilment for people on your team. As a team member, it is important to stay in a zone that invigorates your energy.

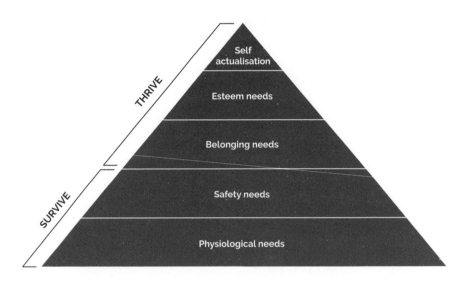

Maslow proposed that you should be mindful of *five* needs that are important for people to first survive, then to grow and thrive. When you consciously focus on any of these in your day-to-day interactions with your team, they will experience the impact as empathy, emanating from someone who knows how important personal fulfilment is for people who give their all at work. These five human needs take you from a focus on basic survival right through to what it means to thrive.

1. Physiological Needs

This first need is about basic survival. Someone who lost their job during COVID may have worried about basic needs: 'Where am I going to live? How am I going to feed my family?' For homeless people and families, these questions are pertinent each and every day. While most of us have never been homeless, you can empathise with the mental fatigue of having to worry about basic needs to survive day to day out on the streets. During scenarios like COVID, especially when the lockdowns were announced, you saw the long lines grow in front of supermarkets as people panicked about whether they had enough of the basic staples in place to live comfortably through an uncertain period of time. It is no different in America when a hurricane is pending; the first thing to go is toilet paper. Then the bread shelves empty, followed by other staples, including water, milk and, oddly enough, chocolates. As we all know, food can be comforting during periods of high stress, as evidenced by those of us who put on a few kilos during lockdown.

One very important thing to keep your eye on in a crisis scenario, and increasingly so in everyday life, are the consequences associated with fatigue. Prior to the word 'pandemic' becoming a part of our lives, an epidemic was considered a big deal. The World Health Organization lists insomnia as a global epidemic, exacerbated by phones, tablets and devices that make us more accessible 24/7. To put the perils of insomnia in proper context, the UN considers sleep deprivation as a form of torture. In those extreme conditions, it is used specifically to break people down — mentally, emotionally and physically. If you have ever pushed yourself to the brink of exhaustion, you can relate to the impact it has on your whole persona.

The World Health Organization lists insomnia as a global epidemic, exacerbated by phones, tablets and devices that make us more accessible 24/7.

While no humane employer would ever deprive people of sleep intentionally, it is easy to lose sight of how pervasive work has become and how the choice to sacrifice sleep may actually be worn as a badge of honour in some work cultures. To the contrary, the research tells us that only one in 40 people can sustain living on six hours or less of sleep each night. The great majority of us still require between seven and eight hours of sleep nightly to perform at our best. A person who has gone for six days on only four hours of sleep each night will show the same impairment as someone who is legally drunk. Increase that to 10 days and the person will resemble someone three times over the legal alcohol limit. To experience chronic fatigue is both unhealthy and unsafe.

As a leader, you can show empathy by keeping an eye on what may seem like unyielding stressors and increased fatigue on your team over extended periods of time. For everyone who had to toggle between family and work pressures associated with COVID, it was clear what toll prolonged stress and mounting fatigue can have on personal effectiveness. That initial surge of adrenaline was followed by a gradual and slowing capacity to maintain pace, which culminated in lower energy levels as the year progressed. The first rung on Maslow's hierarchy certainly became real for many people in 2020. And it will be even more pertinent in the years to follow, yet another reason to bolster resilience to help people cope with frequent and unpredicted change.

2. Safety and Security

At the second level of Maslow's hierarchy sits the need for safety and security, which is about keeping yourself and others safe from psychological or physical harm. These needs include having adequate shelter, employment and job security, law and order, health and wellbeing — many of the same components of a safe work environment. If people do not feel safe in a particular setting, their primary focus will be on mitigating any risk to themselves before they can focus on the higher-level needs in Maslow's hierarchy.

During the COVID lockdowns, some employers and team leaders had to deal with the very real scenario of team members who worked from home with partners who were not coping well with the stress. In some cases, the stress between partners accelerated into emotional and physical abuse, so much so that some employers made the option of working from the office a viable alternative to the home setting. While having more time together during COVID was bonding for many families, for others it was a source of strain and heightened tension. As a leader, showing empathy in this kind of scenario does not require you to intervene into personal decisions that any employee might have to make. But giving them the time and space to sort through their options can make a big difference to how they work their way through.

In the first instance, it helps them to simply know that you understand what they are going through.

Bullying scenarios also qualify as threats to safety and security. Bullying is a common tactic used by people who are insecure about their leadership, who view a different opinion as a threat to their status, and who favour an autocratic rather than collaborative approach with their teams and peers. There is some substance to the belief that people who bully others were once bullied themselves, even if they haven't yet connected the dots, as in the case story of Tom Hartman who didn't 'suffer fools gladly'. If you tolerate bullying in your workplace, it will have severe and costly repercussions, the least of which will be sustainable damage to the organisation's brand and reputation in the eyes of prospective employees and customers. Talented employees who have options will not tolerate a bullying scenario for long. There are no rational gains associated with asking people to work in a setting where they feel unsafe or under threat for speaking their minds or doing what they believe is the right thing. Bullying always ends in a bad place. It is the antithesis of what we expect from an empathetic leader. The parallels to a one-term Trump presidency could not be any clearer.

There are no rational gains associated with asking people to work in a setting where they feel unsafe or under threat for speaking their minds or doing what they believe is the right thing.

Increasingly, another priority in organisations has been on wellbeing. The wellness component requires just as much focus on psychological safety in the workplace as there has been on physical safety. In fact, both go hand in hand, like the consequences of fatigue and sleep deprivation. Anxiety and depressive disorders spiked during the height of COVID, which put leaders in the position of helping to seek outside resources for people who struggled more than most. Some companies are lackadaisical around health and safety measures, compared to those who use symbolism and clout to convey the importance of sending every person safely home to their families each and every day. Employees appreciate knowing that their safety and security are a top priority.

With virtual work having become a reality post-COVID, we can expect to see workplace flexibility factor in more as a viable way to ensure psychological and physical wellbeing for employees. By cutting back on day-to-day rush-hour travel and using reasonable criteria to determine which meetings can be held virtually and which are best to hold in person, this will certainly translate into greater efficiency and productivity with the side benefits of people feeling less tired and drained, not to mention fewer accidents caused by fatigued drivers on the roads. In a world where the lines between work and home have blurred significantly, giving people more flexibility to manage their time is empowering, a display of compassionate empathy that conveys trust in them to manage the balance between competing priorities.

3. The Need to Belong

The third human need is for love and belonging, which loads on our hard wiring as mammals to fit in, feel appreciated and be loved. We typically reserve love for our personal sphere of life, although it is clearly tangible in small businesses and family businesses, where people are either related or very close friends. We all know how love can get in the way in professional relationships, particularly within a chain-of-command scenario, where it is impossible to maintain objectivity about someone who you are romantically involved with. I am always amazed by how two people in a workplace love affair put on blinders, ostensibly to distort reality and minimise attention to themselves, all the while drawing everyone in with loads of speculation about what is really going on. From Maslow's vantage, he was more focused on platonic love, where the connection is not sensual, but more about a deep bond or connection based on purpose, e.g., soldiers at war who are intimately connected by their willingness to die for a cause.

We typically reserve love for our personal sphere of life, although it is clearly tangible in small businesses and family businesses, where people are either related or very close friends.

Love needs aside, the need to belong is very real for most people. I am drawn to one of the primary reasons why people join street gangs, or even sign up with terrorist groups on the other side of the world. It is because many of them have experienced rejection from mainstream society, deemed unacceptable as 'one of us'. These are often people who don't fit in well around 'established' norms where conformity is required. They sit on the fringe, sometimes in defiance, looking for like-minded souls who crave a sense of home and feeling appreciated for what they bring. Unlike some companies where employees' contributions are taken for granted, street gangs are very explicit about ways in which their members can and do add value, each and every day. The human need to belong is not to be denied. Until the advent of EQ and under the old management paradigm, the inference behind this need was *either adjust to the way we do things around here or leave*. The new reality is that everyone brings something of value to benefit the collective purpose.

As a leader, it helps if you are across this particular need with a greater sense of purpose. There is an inherent tension in life between the need to 'fit in' and the need to 'stand out'. To a huge extent, how people manage this tension across time will ultimately determine their personality and the impact they will have in life. Because of the human need to affiliate, there is definitely a stronger gravitational pull in the direction of fitting in with the team or larger group. Sometimes the need to belong — that desire to fit in and be accepted — can pull a person off centre, akin to Emirhan deciding that it was okay for the team to change his name to 'M' for their convenience. Working in the Wall Street bubble, I listened to Eminem every morning in my car on the way to work, a way to rev up the angry and aggressive juices that enabled me to survive and feel valued in a work environment where there were two categories of people — winners and losers. Back then, I compromised my own personal values in order to fit in and be liked by the brass. That kind of scenario is never sustainable.

The human need to belong should not require people to live in either First or Third Circle, where they feel unsafe to be their authentic selves. Second Circle is where that sense of belonging really happens, where there is a healthy balance between fitting in and standing out. Yes, there may be ways in which 'we do things around here' that are a part of our heritage and brand. But those ways should lead to a sense of personal fulfilment with a rewarding and positive energy, rather than people feeling they have to shrink or expand their personas in order to be accepted. Leaders should spend more time helping people to stand out for what they bring with their true persona. The case story of Theo, the youngest member of the team, is a perfect example of how fulfilling it is to know that *belonging* comes with being able to make a difference congruent with your personal values. With the younger generation, the need to belong comes with an important caveat: *Please allow me to bring my voice.* That is difficult to do if 'belonging' requires people to be on mute.

When you tell someone how they have made a positive difference, this goes to the heart of engagement and empathy. When you criticise a person constantly for what they do wrong, it deprives them of the basic need to belong and be needed. Whether in a business or a group, it feels good to be needed, to feel welcomed. It feels good to belong. It's largely an intuitive thing and you know exactly the moment when you finally do belong.

4. The Need for Esteem

A good friend told me a story about when he moved into a new role as division leader at a large retailer. He was new to the company and about to take on an intact team who were eager to learn from his experiences in the UK and Asia. The team were all ready for a change and open to what he was bringing to help lift results. At the beginning of my friend's first week, he asked one of the senior members of his team to help him prepare for a presentation to the board four days later, an opportunity to land a favourable first impression with the directors. Over that week, my friend worked closely with the team member, whom he found to be very giving of her time with loads of helpful insights and perspective. His knowledge of the business grew rapidly over those four days, as well as his confidence in forming some early hypotheses about where to focus. He was grateful for how the team member dropped everything to help him climb the

He was grateful for how the team member dropped everything to help him climb the learning curve as quickly as possible.

learning curve as quickly as possible. As it turned out, the presentation to the board went well, with specific feedback about how impressive his knowledge of the business was after only one week. My friend was stoked about how well things had gone.

Immediately following the presentation, he dropped by the desk of the woman who had helped him prepare, to extend a warm 'thanks' and appreciation for the role she played in a very successful outcome. One minute into the conversation, he was flabbergasted when she jumped up from her seat and dashed away in tears. My friend didn't know what to do, worried that he had somehow offended her. He went back to his desk to figure out what to do. Within a few minutes, she re-emerged and walked over to his desk to explain her reaction. What she told my friend both captivated and disturbed him. She told him that it had been a very long time since any manager had paid her a compliment about anything. She was surprised at her own reaction when she teared up and then ran off. She told him that she felt overwhelmed by his positive comments. My friend was astonished by the gripping reality that this woman was literally starving for affirmation. Like a plant in a drought, suddenly infused with drenching rain, she felt overwhelmed. When my friend later discussed the whole scene with his boss, she said to him, 'that's why you're here.' A heartfelt 'thank you' can mean the world to a person who comes to work each day simply wanting to make a difference. When you validate people for who they are and what they bring, it has huge impact on their self-esteem. We sometimes forget that humans thrive on affirmation.

The need for esteem is very real — for your kids, your partner, your team, your peers and colleagues, and your manager. A heartfelt 'thanks' and telling someone how they made a positive difference can go a long way toward making their day, even their week, sometimes their whole year. Is there someone in your life who could benefit from some affirmation right now?

Into my eighteenth year as a New Zealander, 'tall poppy syndrome' is still alive and well. It is a cultural nuance some take pride in, while others see it as a drag on the confidence of New Zealanders to assert leadership from the forefront, whether that be around entrepreneurship or leading on a global stage (such as our success fighting COVID-19), rather than steering quietly from behind. For me personally, the humility of Kiwis spoke to my heart during my early years down under. I found it to be endearing, leaving no doubt about the motive or intent of the team, which is to make a difference for the collective good — without all the personal grandstanding. The All Blacks exemplify humility at its best, where the emphasis is on team unity and an ethos that mitigates self-absorption.

As yet another of life's wonderful paradoxes, any strength played to excess will become a liability at some point. Humility is a beautiful attribute, but it should be balanced with a good dose of esteem. It is important for individuals to feel good about what they bring to the team and why their contributions are valued — how they have made a difference to the team's success. For anyone who has been genuinely acknowledged for making a difference, it fuels their desire to do more, to give more. This is why recognition ceremonies are important, whether at a primary school 'prize giving' with your eight-year-old who is beaming from ear to ear, or at a corporate gala where hundreds have gathered to acknowledge individual and team achievements.

The need for esteem is really important to a person's confidence. When you constantly say negative things to a person, it erodes their sense of worth and any value they might potentially bring to the table. In our fast-paced world with constant distractions and shorter conversations, 'cutting to the chase' means that you are more likely to focus on those things that are not going well, rather than those that are. As leaders, we sometimes forget that people really do benefit from an occasional dose of positivity. If you constantly drop in on a person to remind them of yet another mistake they have made or something else they did wrong, it will have a negative impact on how they feel about themselves, their work and you. People keep their guard up when they are constantly in a defensive mode over what they may have done wrong. Like all mammals, humans thrive on psychological fuel that comes in the form of positive reinforcement.

Empathy 101. Practise saying 'thanks' more often to the people around you, perhaps taking a few minutes every day to pull a person or two aside simply to tell them how they made a positive difference with a particular outcome. The sentiment must be genuine in order for the recipient to absorb it as heartfelt. If you don't mean it, then don't say it. But if you do mean it, watch the difference it can make in that person's energy level and how engaged they become with their work. Ultimately, healthy self-esteem correlates strongly with a person feeling acknowledged, affirmed and appreciated for who they are and what they bring to the team. At its best, self-esteem is a beautiful feeling of loving who you are and knowing that you have made a difference in life.

As leaders, we sometimes forget that people really do benefit from an occasional dose of positivity.

5. Self-Actualisation

At the top and fifth rung on Maslow's hierarchy is the need to self-actualise, reflected by a person who is driven by a higher sense of purpose, often connected to strong values and principles about how they choose to live and lead. People who are connected to their personal WHY make choices based on what they believe will make the biggest difference to serve the greater good. In a business context, strong employee engagement is driven by people believing that the impact of their work is larger than a pay cheque.

When I practised as a psychotherapist, it was not uncommon for people to experience a certain angst in life toward their mid-40s, often referred to as a 'mid-life crisis'. Typically, in the fifth decade of life, the tectonic plates that define your psyche start to move around a bit, where you are less idealistic about life and more practical when it comes to mapping out your trajectory, based largely on insights and wisdom gained from your personal highs and lows over a few decades. Life experiences really do translate into perspective, often experienced as 'intuition', where you are inclined to go with your gut rather than a more rational choice when facing a major decision, such as leaving a partner, changing career path, or reprioritising quality over quantity in how you live your life. Can you imagine what it would be like to deliberate whether to change your gender to lead a more fulfilled life? As a parent or sibling to someone facing that choice, your empathy would be vital.

The classic image of 'mid-life crisis' once took on a negative undertone, such as people standing in judgement of a middle-aged guy who leaves his wife for a woman half his age and then rides off with her in a new, red convertible Mustang. At surface level, that image may seem superficial, perhaps someone who has come a bit unhinged, maybe working his way through a few issues. At a deeper level, it may reflect someone who realises that he hasn't been happy for most of his life, has consistently prioritised work over relationships and has operated on the notion that 'saving for retirement' is better than 'living for today'. Mid-life adjustments are often viewed with judgement, less so with empathy, even though they are as normal as life itself. It takes a decent chunk of time in life to get to know the person in the mirror well enough to have an honest conversation about the best path ahead.

> It takes a decent chunk of time in life to get to know the person in the mirror well enough to have an honest conversation about the best path ahead.

I made a mid-life adjustment in my early 40s that required me to disrupt the lives of those I loved the most, in order to navigate a path where I could live a more complete life for myself. My family showed considerable empathy for me when I made the choice to disrupt what I perceived as 'tradition' and come out as a gay man. I personally experienced what it feels like when the tectonic plates shift in your psyche, when I finally realised that it was not sustainable, no longer healthy, for me to remain an impostor. That was my first 'up close' and personal experience with self-actualisation, when the last rung on Maslow's hierarchy became real for me.

I encourage you to watch Simon Sinek's TED Talk: 'The Power of Why'. Sinek introduces a three-looped 'golden circle' that highlights the importance of a person or team going inward to connect with a strong sense of purpose, then moving back outward to shape how and what they deliver to the world. The premise is that your WHY will drive your HOW and WHAT. To self-actualise is ultimately about finding your purpose in life. Some may even describe it as a personal sense of destiny, something you believe you were born to do, where you invigorate others through your natural strengths and passions.

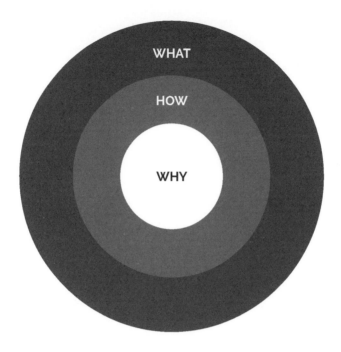

More often than not, your purpose is wired to some natural or inherent strength that fuels your psyche, not only because you are great at it, but also because people love it when you are in that zone. Some of us are wired aesthetically, whether that be through art or music or writing, or designing homes and buildings, laying out a city grid, cultivating a garden or creating culinary delights people can't take their eyes off. Aesthetic geniuses are all around us. Other people are wired differently, to go deep with their focus, where they are energised by pulling things apart, dissecting stuff, seeing the interplay between all the parts across the system, then reconstructing them in a better way. And then there are people who are energised by the stratospheres, to push their thinking upward and outward, gifted with the ability to envision and articulate what the future looks like. We call this the bigger picture, which usually comes with aspiration, inspiration and loads of energy.

We are all wired differently around our strengths and passions. They come alive in us when we are kids, whether through sports, music, art, design, or the gift of the gab. Some people nail their sweet spot earlier in life, giving themselves more runway to maximise those strengths, an important part of personal fulfilment. For most people, self-awareness grows gradually across time and usually culminates in a personal reckoning (getting yourself more grounded), which may take you in a different direction. Your personal WHY is integral to who you are. It takes a fair degree of life experience, personal reflection and a decent amount of self-awareness for a person to land squarely on their ultimate purpose in life. It also requires a good dose of honesty about who you are.

Be Human. If you believe that Abraham Maslow was onto something nearly 80 years ago with his views on what humans require to thrive, this may prompt you to think more consciously about how to help someone on your team, or in your life, reach a greater sense of fulfilment. Positivity, optimism and encouragement make a huge difference in the quality of life for others. People are more personally engaged with you when they believe you want them to succeed. As a leader, you have direct impact on the energy of your team. When people are in survival mode, their energy is largely insular rather than outward. When people are thriving, you can feel their energy emanating outward on so many frequencies. Yet another reason why *needing other people* is important to a leader's success. Your role is to help people belong, especially by bringing their authentic selves to work each day. It is easier for them to do this if you value their perspective. When you put pressure on yourself to be the perfect boss, it breaks connection. The vibe you send out is, 'your input is optional'. To grow your empathy, learn how to need other people more. Take the pressure off yourself to be omnipotent.

Positivity, optimism and encouragement make a huge difference in the quality of life for others. People are more personally engaged with you when they believe you want them to succeed.

16

BUILDING YOUR EMPATHY TOOLKIT: THE ART OF STORYTELLING

Universal to Humans. Social anthropologists describe storytelling as one of the major ways by which the earliest humans communicated their tribal lineage and conveyed cultural norms and values prior to recorded history. There are the perennial images of cavemen and women gathered around drawings (rock art) etched into stone walls, one person standing and orating while others sit around the fire and follow the story through the power of their vivid imaginations. It is human to imagine. It is human to envision. Stories grab us. They take us in, transport us to another place and allow us to live vicariously through another person's experience.

As highlighted in Chapter 5, we are wired for empathy and there is no better vehicle than a story to envision yourself in the shoes of another person, to literally feel their pain. Stories infuse energy into an empathetic response, best described as a 'feeling', which most people can relate to at a very personal level. There is nothing like a good story to get other people in the same emotional zone with you. Because our limbic (emotive) brain does not have the capacity for language, it is often difficult to explain why another person's story has moved you to the point of tears, or even rage. Stories touch us all in gripping ways. The connection with the other person is visceral.

Dr Martin Luther King's famous speech, 'I Have a Dream', was him talking about a dream he envisioned when America would be unified in a land where black and white kids could play together, to go to school together. That speech is one of the most compelling examples of the power of inspiration. His words galvanised white and black Americans to take a stand around the importance of working together to build a more inclusive society. A story helps to put a vision into the heads of people who want to believe in something that is deeper than the toil of their hard work. Humans are fuelled by inspiration and stories are a great way to fuel more positive energy across the team.

Stories Build Wisdom. Human knowledge and intellect, the way we make meaning about everyday life, is based largely on stories. We learn and adapt through stories, largely because we all lead storied lives. Stories are most often based on experiential learning, where you, or someone close to you, have gone through a particular experience first-hand. Whether it be a person who once suffered a terrible loss, or someone who accomplished something huge in their life, reliving the experience through story enables them to gain insights, perspective and even wisdom. Telling a story is helpful to the storyteller because it enables them, across time, to shape their thinking around specific narrative structures that resonate more deeply with an audience. In fact, a good story will often mirror how humans learn best, such as keeping things simple, the rule of three and summarising key points. The more often you tell a story, the more confident you become in landing it with impact. An audience is more likely to remember facts better if they are packaged as smaller versions of a larger story. A Stanford research study showed that statistics, when presented alone, have a retention rate of only 5–10 per cent, but when coupled with anecdotes, the retention rate rises to 65–70 per cent. To that end, storytelling can supplement analytical thinking, a good way to help people encode data and facts that might otherwise seem disparate or irrelevant.

In essence, to tell and hear a good story is fundamental to how humans live, learn and adapt. I can attest to this personally. My thinking and passion grew tremendously around the topic of authenticity after friends encouraged me to tell my story in a TED Talk about what it was like to serve as a closeted gay military officer. The essence of that story was how I went too far in my quest to be a 'perfect' man. Although I had not anticipated the impact, the more I told the story, the more real and emotional it became for me. Telling that story numerous times since 2015 has helped me to shape my own views and beliefs about the detrimental impact of impostor syndrome. Through a simple story, the topic of authenticity became personal for me, no longer hypothetical. And it became real for others too.

A strong way to show empathy is to share and hear more personal stories about the highs and lows that come with being human. Storytelling has and will continue to be an inherent part of our evolution. Make it easier for people to talk about their own experiences and what they have learned, and are still learning from them. It is also a great thing to reinforce with young kids to help them talk about experiences and what they learned from them. Each time they tell the story, you will hear their wisdom grow a bit more.

The Gift of the Gab. Some people have exceptional verbal aptitude where they use words and language to influence people, often to their advantage. Unfortunately, there are people out there with sociopathic traits who exploit others through their gift of the gab. Such people are likely to be charming and intelligent. This is where your intuition serves you well. Your gut usually tells you when the connection is not genuine.

Then there are some people who draw you in because of their authenticity, often conveyed by their ability to paint a picture and create music through their words. This is someone you like because of the

way they make you feel, largely through conversations. As is the case with people who are in frequent conversations, you learn a lot about each other through stories. Some people are exceptional at it. They have a name: *Ra-con-teur*, from the French word meaning 'to recount'.

A raconteur is a professional storyteller. It is not a practised thing, but rather feels more natural and far more real. Character plays a big role. On the US political front, Ronald Reagan was superb with stories, as were Bill Clinton and Barack Obama, all three who were two-term presidents with favourable appeal. In New Zealand, I have been moved by the stories of Tame Iti, a Māori activist, speaker and Māori Party candidate, who gave a compelling TEDx Talk about mana in 2015. I had the pleasure of hearing Sir John Key speak in my early days in New Zealand. Politics aside, but even when they were on the table, it was impressive to hear the Prime Minister weave in his business and life experiences into stories that helped shed light on how his own views and perspectives had been shaped. In his stories, I could sense his strong ethos. And I really enjoy the stories that Jacinda Ardern tells about New Zealand when she is on a late-night talk show in another part of the world. Her stories about growing up in New Zealand embody Kiwi humility, all the while reinforcing how strong we are as a people. Whether on the political or business front, or even your neighbour next door, there are great storytellers all around you.

Raconteur 101. Lead with character, be authentic and strive to make a difference through a story. That is the starting point. On the opposite page are three key things to focus on if you want to inspire and motivate people through stories. They are anchored around the timeless proofs of rhetorical persuasion, recently updated in a 2018 TED Talk by Frances Frei where she modernises the three proofs as separate points on the 'trust triangle'. Along with authenticity and logic, empathy is imperative to establish trust and a strong connection with another person or group. This certainly is the case with storytelling. For your story to resonate deeply, you need all three.

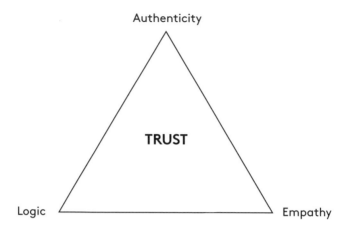

1. AUTHENTICITY
Be real
- Personal stories that have shaped your perspective help to connect the 'real you' with the group. People *feel with* a storyteller who shares a personal story. You project a stronger energy when you give people a window into your life.
- Model vulnerability. It is a turn-off for people who perceive that you are a superhero who lives in a different world than theirs. People relate better to stories that reinforce human imperfection, where you have learned lessons through hard times.
- Every now and then in a story, it helps to position yourself as the antagonist who learned a powerful lesson through self-discovery.

Know your audience
- Do your homework. If you are not a member of the team, then learn a reasonable bit about the group and find a way to weave in parallels to their world.
- Context is everything, so be prepared to alter your story depending on where the group's collective head is. Know why they are there, gauge their temperament and know their expectations.
- Trust your gut on how much leverage you get with humour.
- Your credibility is enhanced if the group believes that you know them well enough. This is easier if you are one of them. Be sure to connect key pivot points in your story with parallels to their world.

Make sure they know you

- If you are on the team, this is less likely a problem, but not always. People listen based on their perceived credibility of your story's relevance to them, there in the moment, with their full attention.
- If not on the team, be prepared to take a few minutes to put some context around your background, particularly related to a few stories you may tell. People listen with a different ear if you are confident to talk about your professional background. Worn well, bling matters.
- In a story, tell people something about the personal impact an experience had on you, even if second-hand.

Emotion connects when genuine

- Never feel bad about purposefully going into Third Circle if you are truly passionate about something.
- Living through life's challenges means that you occasionally push through grief of some kind, like the loss of loved ones, jobs and an income, life stability, sometimes status. There is pain in grief. Don't be afraid to show it.
- In a story, tears are okay. Anger is okay. Hope is okay. Emotion is okay as long as it is genuine. The group or audience will know if you are bullshitting them.

2. EMPATHY

Be present

- Minimise all distractions — those behind you, those around you, those in front of you. Be in the moment. Otherwise, you will come across as robotic.
- When telling a story, strive for Second Circle. In First Circle, you are bringing very little energy. In Third Circle, you are bringing too much energy. Keep a good read on which circle you are in.
- The more you tell the same story, the more rote it may sound to the group, no different than what famous singers have to remind themselves before they go out on stage: sing it like it is the very first time.

Listen with your eyes, see with your ears

- The older and wiser you get, learn to listen more to your gut — especially through your eyes. Sustain eye contact with a few people to gauge their connection to the story and where it may need to go to bring them back in. Not only can you feel the energy from the group, you can also see it.
- Your ears should be turned on full volume when telling a story. Confusion or detachment is usually conveyed through silence. You can see it through your ears, the same as laughter. Is it real or stilted?
- Two of your primary senses play a big role in informing you to make an adjustment if a story needs to be shortened or lengthened.

Wear their shoes

- Understand their headspace. Whether through your personal experiences, or those of others, connect your story to where they currently are. How is the narrative relevant to their starting point?
- Is this a story to ground them in their current reality? Key to personal resilience, people often value a story that reinforces the need to accept reality as it is. The COVID-19 scenario would have brought this home in a very real way for many people.
- Is the story intended to create a healthy tension between their current reality and a vision of how things can be? From inspiration comes aspiration. Do you sense that the person or group could use a decent injection of optimism?

The rule of three

- Is your intent to infuse all three forms of empathy into the story, or would it be best to highlight just one?
- With cognitive empathy, the main character might have an 'a-ha' moment, such as hearing about a colleague's experience and imagining how terrible that would feel. It helps the audience to appreciate what it means to understand.
- With emotional empathy, the main character is touched at a deeper level, where another person's experience is the catalyst for them

to pull insights through to a healthier level. Are there benefits to feeling another person's pain? On occasion, bring that through in story.

- In most stories, compassionate empathy resonates at the deepest level for people, often where there is a hero.

3. LOGIC
Be relevant

- Why are you telling us this story? How is it relevant to the discussion we are having and what our goals are at this meeting? Before you start the story, it is helpful to give people some brief context on its relevance. Connect it to a point that you just made, or signal its relevance to an insight you will share once done. It goes back to the importance of context. If the story is not resonating within a couple of minutes, you will start to lose the group.
- Both you and the story should be relevant to the team's mindset and where things need to go.
- Not only should your story be relevant, but so should you. That goes back to what the team or group knows about your background and experience. They lean in more if you have been immersed in a situation that gives credence to where you are trying to take them.

Get on the same channel

- Some people are wired for the bigger picture, where they are energised by pushing their thinking upward and outward. Other groups may be more analytical by the very nature of their work and natural aptitude to immerse themselves in detail. Tailor your story to where the logic is most likely to resonate as you take them along with you.
- Aesthetics are important. Some people live in a more colourful world in terms of what may resonate with them, which gives you more latitude to add some pizzazz to your story, akin to adding hot sauce on top of a pizza. With the right person or group, strive to open up the energy with more colour.
- Mind your humour. Comedians tell loads of stories where they constantly infuse humour to either break the tension or to reinforce

something everyone can relate to and laugh about. Even around a painful story, humour can help to illuminate a lesson learned. But there is such a thing as 'too soon'. Be mindful of when humour might backfire.

Land the story

- Have a point. We have all been there on the other side of a story that is wandering between different stratospheres. This is when your eyes and ears can serve you well.
- Stick to the three-minute rule. You can cover a lot of ground in 180 seconds. If you plan to tell more than one story, the three-minute rule sets a cadence for the group to trust that you will keep things on point. Always leave them wanting more rather than less.
- Link back to key points in your presentation or from the conversation. What may be clear in your own mind may still be a bit fuddled for someone who is processing your story and trying to make the connection. Help to land it for them.

Four Story Archetypes. As a storyteller, while it is important to sharpen the three elements on the trust triangle to have a strong connection with the group, you should also think  about the type of story that would make the biggest difference. Across the span of civilisation, story types have largely fallen within the realm of four major archetypes, a term that implies that, as humans, we are instinctively and emotionally drawn toward certain constructs, shaped by our ancestors' experiences that have evolved into what we call the 'human psyche'. *Hope* is one of those archetypes. It is fuelled by a sense of triumph, where the story may help the person or group to envision what it is like to prevail and kick some serious ass, especially against the odds, to land in a better place. Or is your story about a person or group working through *despair*, perhaps immersed in it, needing to find the will to persevere, keep everyone focused and remain positive? Most people can relate to having been there in life. Or the story may be about a person or team who had a personal *reckoning*, having lived through an event that shook the very foundation of who they were, where they came out on the other side with deeper values and priorities. A fourth story type is about *change*, which every person listening to your story can relate to personally, particularly the angst that comes along with stretching yourself from one curve to the next.

As a leader, you might find it helpful to think through each of the four archetypes and determine whether you have a couple of robust stories that may make a difference to a person or team in one of those particular zones. Following is a sample of each story archetype.

1. Hope

In his book, *The Audacity of Hope*, Barack Obama writes about the incredulity of how he, or anyone else for that matter, could have predicted two decades earlier that a man whose identity as *African-American* (the son of a Kenyan father and American mother) would ever be elected President of the United States of America. Living in New Zealand, the first democratic nation to extend voting rights to women in 1893 with three female prime ministers since then, I find it astonishing that it took 244 years of American political history to elect a woman, Kamala Harris, to serve as either president or vice president.

In America, I grew up wearing a lens, one shaped by history, that you could only become president if you were a white man. In my lifetime, there was Eisenhower, Kennedy, Johnson, Nixon, Ford, Carter, Reagan, Bush #1, Clinton and Bush #2. And then in 2008, along came Barack Obama, an anomaly, a striking and relatively young black man who was well-educated, charismatic, grounded in decent values and who resonated instantly with a compelling energy across the colourful tapestry of America. At first, I gave him little chance to succeed. There had been other black presidential candidates in my lifetime, but none of them serious contenders to be elected as the nominee for their party. Many people of colour in my generation had conceded that the best you can do is strive for the House or Senate in federal politics, but don't even think about running for the top seat. The president of America, a position that some refer to as the most powerful in the world, was reserved for a white man.

Barack Obama will always be one of the most memorable presidents in US history because of his relevance to the archetype of hope. As humans, we thrive on hope to better ourselves. We count on hope to take ourselves to a better place. Hope rejuvenates the spirit and soul with positivity and optimism. It broadens our horizons, akin to what it feels like to see someone break through a glass ceiling. Like many black people in America and around the world, I cried tears of joy that night in 2008 when Obama was first elected. It was such a feeling of liberation for so many people, like a huge blanket being lifted from our sense of belonging. The best way to describe the feeling was one of hope, one that I had never experienced before at such a macro sphere in the realm of diversity and inclusion. I can imagine that many girls and women in America, and around the world, felt that same hope when Hillary Clinton was nominated in 2016, yet another glass ceiling having been shattered. I love that my daughters and grandsons are growing up in an America where they can now envision themselves being led by bold aspirations with no ceilings that hover over their dreams.

The archetype of hope invigorates the human spirit around what is possible, what can be, why you should never give up and why it is important to persevere. People who reach self-actualisation have often relied on hope to keep themselves focused, motivated and committed. If you know a person or team striving to break into new ground for the first time, even against all odds, a compelling story of hope and possibility can make a huge difference to their psychological energy. From the experiences of your life, are there a few stories that exemplify the power of hope?

2. Despair

The opposite of hope is despair, when you have to work your way through pain, or some type of personal struggle, that has pushed you to a point of reckoning. I have certainly danced around with this archetype in my life, in fact a good deal of my life before I decided to become a whole person, no longer afraid of being rejected for who I am. There is pain in despair, as everyone can personally relate to at some level, regardless of social status. In the moment, pain can hurt big time, especially when things are coming to a crescendo, often causing a person or team to experience a sense of pessimism and self-doubt. We have all been there at different points in our lives and careers. Despair would be the equivalent of feeling like you have run out of options with nowhere to turn. It is literally that feeling of having your back to the wall, where you finally have to deal with what is in front of you.

There is pain in despair, as everyone can personally relate to at some level, regardless of social status.

I share my story about the experience of what it was like to 'come out' because I want it to resonate with people who may be stuck in a situation that has started to push in on them, sometimes to their detriment. In life and at work, people can relate to a sense of mounting pressures, often brought on by their own doing, exacerbated by denying or delaying decisions that are difficult to make, but are essential for them to be able to turn the story around.

Dwight, a good friend in America, lost his wife and seven-year-old son in a plane crash in 1989. He and his oldest son were not on the flight and, within the flash of a moment, their lives were altered forever, both of them having to work their way through grief and deep despair. There they were, a grieving father and his young son, having to grab hold of something to give them hope. For my friend, he relied on two things to help him get through that patch of darkness. One was his religious faith, which gave him peace that he would one day be reunited with his wife and son. The second was knowing that he had to really be there, fully present and strong, for his 10-year-old son who was grieving the loss of his mum and little brother. A sense of purpose really makes a huge difference when you are pushing through despair, one that my friend could relate to more than most people will ever have to. His faith and strong sense of purpose helped him climb out of a deep hole to find a healthier place in life.

Dwight would eventually remarry and create new happiness in his life, only to then lose his oldest son in a motorcycle accident two decades later. For many people, that would have pushed them over the edge of despair, either to withdraw inward or become cynical about faith in God or a deeper sense of purpose or meaning to life. Even after losing the three people who were once his whole world, Dwight held true to his faith. He and his wife relocated to California to live within a few miles of his son's widow and their five-year-old grandson, who they absolutely adore. Their story personifies what it is like to feel despair, to truly understand the struggle to hold onto hope in the face of personal pain. It also personifies the power of hope, fuelled by optimism and positivity, both of which correlate with resilience. Dwight's first wife and two sons are gone, but he can feel their presence through the joy and laughter of his grandson. For me, personally, there has never been a more gripping example of the power of hope over despair.

3. Reckoning

A person going through a reckoning is experiencing a fundamental shift in their mental models about how the world works. And how they fit into that world, perhaps with a much different sense of purpose. A personal reckoning essentially speaks to a transition in your life, typically sparked by an event that causes you to reassess your values and priorities. Earlier in the book, I referenced the story about the extraordinary friendship between Daryl Davis, a black musician, and Robert Kelly, who was once an Imperial Wizard of the Ku Klux Klan. For both men, and for the hundreds of other KKK members who eventually denounced their membership, their stories are compelling because they remind us how empathy often entails having to shift your own values around to adapt to a broader reality.

When you consider the strong racial tensions that continue to divide America into its third century, the events that reshaped the lives of Davis and Kelly really do reinforce how a reckoning often has to be deeply personal. Hopefully, some of the rioters who stormed the US Capitol just before the 2021 presidential inauguration have reflected deeply about democracy and their role in making it more about civility and unity rather than division. Given the role Donald Trump played by rallying his supporters, only to deny any accountability afterwards, it is unlikely that empathy will ever be an arrow in his leadership bow.

At a diversity forum back when I served on the faculty at the US Air Force Academy, a pilot talked about an experience earlier in his career when a group of male pilots, he among them, decided to play a trick on the first ever female pilot in their ranks who would be joining them on a training flight the very next day. They all agreed to place an open can of tuna under her seat in the flight deck, then proceeded to speculate what that smell could be, some going so far as to ask her if she had showered before coming on board. This pilot was young in his career, the same as Theo in the case story, so he remained silent while the older pilots led the harassment across a four-hour flight. In retrospect, he would learn an invaluable lesson about the perils of complicity. When he told the story, you could feel his conviction. He hated that he had taken part in something so egregious.

He vowed that he would never be silent or complicit again, to signal consent for a group to intentionally offend and exclude another person.

Silence does not make you any less culpable when it comes to the negative impact that harassment can have on another person. In fact, the impact is heightened in some cases, particularly under the weight of a heavy conscience when you know that you have crossed an important line. This was indeed the case for him, before and especially after his two daughters were born. When faced with the reality of raising two daughters in a world where they would have to confront scenarios like the one he participated in, his world view changed significantly. He vowed that he would never be silent or complicit again, to signal consent for a group to intentionally offend and exclude another person. His story was a powerful one to hear, well-received by the young cadets and future officers who could relate to what that experience would have been like for any of their friends to endure. He asked them to put a real person's face onto any intended target of harassment or discrimination, and then to see if it made a difference to whether they chose to sit silently or take action to preserve another person's dignity.

In most cases, change is the catalyst for growth, whether self-induced or through decisions beyond your control.

A personal reckoning can be profound in a person's life. Perhaps you have been there before, where you experienced a shift in your tectonic plates that define who you are as a person. These are powerful stories to tell when a person or team is going through a zone of deep reflection about who they really are and what will define their legacy. Painful or challenging experiences will often take you into a different and better headspace. It helps if you have a long view on life, where pain is often a catalyst for growth. People instinctively relate to the power of a personal reckoning, where you start to draw lines in the sand associated with your values. Across life, those lines get firmer. We have all been there. A story about a reckoning can be powerful for a person or team, even a nation, to hear.

4. Change

The first three story archetypes usually culminate in some degree of change that entails personal or professional growth. In most cases, change is the catalyst for growth, whether self-induced or through decisions beyond your control. In life, you push through multiple challenges, some invigorating and some really tough, an important way to develop character and wisdom. The sigmoid curve reinforces how growth in life entails moving from one learning curve to the next, sometimes by your own design, but often having to rock and roll with the punches. That next curve may be your choice to start or shut down a relationship, or to pursue a new career path, or take some time off, perhaps for the first time in your life, to truly enjoy life. Growth is personal to every person. You can appreciate why empathy makes a difference to someone who has just jumped onto a new curve, especially with some risk. Given how personal stretch and growth can be a vulnerable space for many people, it does help for them to hear and feel support.

I met Georgina Beyer at a leadership forum in 2019. Her story is one that reinforces how a personal reckoning will often lead to a powerful story of change. Beyer is a New Zealand politician and former Labour Party Member of Parliament. She was the world's first openly transgender mayor, as well as the world's first openly transgender Member of Parliament. She speaks with genuine candour about having been among a very small number of former sex workers to hold political office. Many people never have a 'first' in their life story. Beyer has a few firsts, which positions her as a noteworthy example of what it means to not only evolve and grow, but also to literally transform her life. Most people tend to face into incremental change, some never getting anywhere close to a true transformation, which requires a fundamental shift in the lens you have on yourself, your life, your whole world. This is the league that Beyer played in when she scoped out how she would live her life.

Beyer spoke about the connection between her own authenticity and the willingness of people to reciprocate with their support, among them some of the most conservative constituents in New Zealand who backed her because she was genuine with them. After she made the decision to transition as a woman, Beyer learned first-hand the strong relationship between authenticity and empathy. If you are genuine with other people and they sense that you are coming from a good place with the best intent, they overlook the outer layers of who you are, focusing instead on the inner core of what you stand for and why that matters.

As in 1986 when Dame Fran Wilde successfully led legislation to overturn the illegality of being a gay man in New Zealand, MP Beyer followed her moral compass in 2003, when she influenced a number of her peers to legalise prostitution in New Zealand, asking them to move beyond their personal beliefs and to consider the perspective of those people, mostly poor and marginalised women, who risk their health, safety and lives in a sector that will never disappear. Her approach was that we can pretend it doesn't exist, or we can make it safer for everyone. Beyer talked several MPs across the line to vote 'yes' by sharing her personal experience of the dangers she faced as a sex worker and why it would be best to impose safer standards, regulations and safeguards. The final vote was 60 in favour, 59 opposed, with one abstention. Beyer's story is a living example of how your personal example, and your voice, can make a real difference when something really matters to you.

In 2003, it was a story of change and growth that beckoned me to New Zealand. I was drawn to the story of Fonterra, one that started to take shape two years prior to my arrival following the merger of the country's two largest dairy cooperatives, New Zealand Dairy Group and Kiwi Cooperative Dairies,

> *Beyer's story is a living example of how your personal example, and your voice, can make a real difference when something matters to you.*

along with the New Zealand Dairy Board. These three giants agreed to merge their respective assets and strengths to launch the third largest dairy company in the world, which would be responsible for approximately 30 per cent of global dairy exports. I was drawn to this compelling story. I had never worked for a business that would have such a tangible impact on the economic viability of a nation, not just for its shareowners, but with a broader ripple effect. For the first time in my career, I finally understood what 'line of sight' meant. Prior to Fonterra, that terminology was an 'old school' expression that meant that everyone at work could explain how their role makes a difference in the lives of other people, within and beyond the business. In my previous roles with Amoco and Prudential, I was unable to speak to 'line of sight' with such a personal connection. In the early days of

Fonterra, it seemed that every employee had friends or relatives whose lives were directly impacted by the quality of their work. My team showed up every day wanting to make a positive difference for people they knew personally. For those of us who were new to New Zealand, we felt the connection. I had never experienced a deeper sense of personal commitment than in those early days with Fonterra.

The Art of Story. In stories that personify change, you can track the clear links between hope, despair, personal reckoning and growth. In storytelling, this circle is the standard definition of a character arc, which shows how your main character changes over the course of your story. The most common form of character arc is called the *Hero's Journey* — one inspired by a vision to push through hard times, to then have a personal reckoning around those things that really matter, and to ultimately grow and carry new wisdom and perspective into the next chapter. In my lifetime, I have seen LGBTI+ rights evolve to the point where people can be who they need to be, where partners can marry and raise a family, where two dudes holding hands as they walk along are greeted with smiles rather than frowns. In the leadership realm, women ruling the world is a compelling construct when you consider that more cities, states, provinces and nations have more female leaders than ever before in history. This, in itself, is a great story. As Goleman predicted, emotional intelligence prevails. The world will continue to swirl in concentric circles forever.

Do you have some personal stories that would make a real difference in the lives of other people? Being a raconteur is a very important role to play, the true gift of the gab. From despair to hope, to reckoning and change, there is true power in a story.

17

THE LEADERSHIP CHALLENGE

Resilience Matters. As a leader, resilience is a human capability you can build within yourself and others. It became very real for all of us in 2020. Resilience and agility are now required to simply stay in the game with your business. It seems like ages ago when 'management' was the equivalent of stabilising a business model. Now, leading through disruption is the norm. The classic sigmoid curve has compressed business cycles into roughly 18-month waves, where your team either adapts to the changing world around you, or falls off the proverbial cliff. That is no longer a hypothetical proposition, as many business owners and leaders discovered very personally in their first experience with a global pandemic.

A 2015 *Harvard Business Review* article highlighted three factors that comprise resilience, all very pertinent in our lives now. The first factor is being able to accept reality as quickly as possible. It is what it is. The sooner you get there, the quicker you can rebound. The human brain does some phenomenal stuff to protect you from stress, including defence mechanisms such as denial, rationalisation and repression — all intended to keep the pain away. But the reality is, life catches up with you at some point and then you will have to face the challenge. No matter how horrific the scenario, strong leadership up front makes a big difference. Give people the facts as soon as you can so they can manage their lives in response. In psychology, this is called 'locus of control'. The sooner you help people to grasp the current reality, the quicker they can make choices to adapt. Feeling in control of your own life is an important component of empowerment. When it comes to resilience, sooner is always better than later.

The second factor that correlates strongly with resilience is having a deeper meaning to life. You might think of this as keeping things in a broader perspective. When people are anxious or feel vulnerable, there is a natural tendency for them to go inward and downward. Their energy becomes insular, as if in a protective stance. As a leader, you can help people to pull their perspective back upward and outward. The bigger picture offers more viable solutions than when a person is stuck deep in an anxious scenario. There is much more light around the bigger picture and the options begin to open up more broadly. For people who are spiritual, that deeper meaning is often associated with faith, which cannot grow unless it is tested through adversity. In fact, it was Aristotle who coached leaders to seek adversity as a way to grow their ethos (character). Deeper meaning in life makes a difference to your resilience when you are pushing through challenging scenarios.

The third factor is your ability to improvise when things start to unravel in a way you had not predicted. During the COVID lockdowns, people found some amazing and amusing ways to keep their routines going. A news report showed a guy using his two-year-old twin sons as weights as he bench-pressed them into the air while they squealed with glee. Not only was he getting a workout, but it was a fun bonding experience with his boys. Everything from haircuts to makeshift home offices to virtual schooling for the kids — it all opened up some creative solutions to deal with the abrupt shutdown on what we once considered normal. Humour is a good sign you are keeping

things in proper perspective. Your
ability to improvise often comes with
lots of laughs.

*The important thing is to help
the person feel some locus
of control over how things
will unfold in the midst of a
challenging scenario.*

If these three factors resonate with
your own personal experience, you
should consider ways to infuse them
into your coaching conversations: (1)
accept reality as quickly as possible;
(2) focus on the long view for deeper meaning; and (3) turn lemons
into lemonade when you have to. The important thing is to help the
person feel some locus of control over how things will unfold in the
midst of a challenging scenario. Their ability to have some impact on
the direction of travel, even in a minor way, can be energising and
also reinforces the importance of helping people to avoid a sense of
helplessness when they are under pressure.

Inclusion. For people who grew up in the early years of America's
'affirmative action' era, essentially the 1970s and 80s, many of us would
re-write the script to put the 'I' before the 'D'. Inclusion before diversity,
rather than the other way around. Hindsight is always perfect, but we got
the order of the two critical ingredients wrong. By focusing on specific
targets and quotas back then, to bring more women, racial and ethnic
minorities, gays and lesbians into the fold, the noise was largely around
'minorities' who were taking away jobs from qualified white people —
older white, straight men in particular, who felt like they had targets on
their chests. I had never heard the term 'reverse discrimination' before
moving to New Zealand. I learned quickly that the expression was
equivalent to quotas and targets. Whether affirmative action or reverse
discrimination, both words implied that diversity, certainly in the early
days, was perceived as a compliance exercise designed largely to 'tick a
box' as opposed to leaders actively building inclusive team cultures.

Take the analogy of healthy plants in bad soil, made popular by Jack
Welch, former CEO of General Electric, who was iconic for knowing
how to develop talent in his company. If you put healthy seedlings into
unhealthy soil, the end result will not be good. They will eventually
wither and die. Diversity is about the seedlings, akin to bringing in

talented people to make a difference. Inclusion is about the soil, which goes to the heart of a company's culture. If the soil disables people from being authentic and bringing what they have to offer, it is only a matter of time before the plants die. On many fronts, it is very costly to recruit and then lose talented people who cannot thrive in non-inclusive soil. Decades after affirmative action, we now know that, when it comes to staff engagement and its direct impact on performance, the business case for inclusion has never been stronger.

In a nutshell, the essence of inclusion boils down to whether you and the team value authenticity. Yes, many people say they value authenticity, but when put to the test, we are often influenced by both our own conscious and unconscious biases. If you require a cookie cutter approach to how everyone is expected to turn up each day, where everyone has to look, act and sound the same, your team will start to conceal their genuine personas in order to fit in and be accepted. For most people, the gravitational pull to fit in outweighs the pull to stand out, particularly in New Zealand. In Aotearoa, our culture reinforces a quieter and more humble presence, reinforced when your peers turn down the volume on your edge and pull you back into a quieter space if you start to puff up too large. Leaders have to work harder to make it easier for people to bring their voices and to believe that their opinions matter and can make a difference.

If you value inclusion, your goal should be to increase the volume on your team's voice, rather than mute everyone and force them into First Circle, where they are far more compliant than committed. If your team is very quiet and rarely bring their perspective on issues, you should be concerned. They have likely picked up signals, deep and cultural, that suggest that a good employee is a quiet employee, especially if they consider themselves to be a tick in the diversity box. What good is diversity if you have a colourful tapestry of people at your table, but they are all nodding yes to everything you say? Inclusion is a value, something leaders and companies hold as a guiding principle on how they want their teams to feel about their contribution at work. You can put robots on mute. It is unhealthy to mute human beings who are driven by an inherent need to make a difference, important to their sense of esteem.

Below are the 10 tenets of inclusion, which reinforce the analogy of soil and plants and the importance of being explicit about working in a culture where inclusion is more than just a word in your annual report, actively working to create a culture of belonging. Another way to think about the tenets is the ethos that sits under an inclusive culture where people can thrive.

INCLUSION
The 10 Tenets

1. Inclusivity is as human as it gets.
2. Our culture is soil, our people are plants, the crop is our sustainability.
3. In an ecosystem of safety, there are no oppressors or victims.
4. We welcome, value and affirm people who want to belong and make a difference.
5. We appreciate people for their authentic selves, all aligned around common purpose.
6. Leadership is defined by voice and perspective, not by rank.
7. Noisy teams are healthier than quiet teams.
8. Our demography reflects the diversity across and beyond our value chain.
9. We affirm, reward and promote people who support the success of others.
10. We enable our people to thrive.

Clearly, the 'D' is still very important for reasons that are no longer obscure or legislative. Most progressive boards, executive teams and leaders understand that people with diverse backgrounds do bring rich and diverse perspectives to the table, which fuels innovation and drives higher performance. But get the 'I' right first, otherwise your best efforts to promote diversity cannot flourish. To lead with greater empathy, ensure the soil is healthy under your team. Inclusion means that everyone can bring their authentic self and perspective to the table. When the goal is for everyone to be 'all in', nothing is more important than an inclusive culture.

Stretch, Pain and Growth. In any business, you should be worried if you or the team are too comfortable. That is also the case in life, predicated on the natural cycle of the sigmoid curve, an algebraic equation that alerts us to the symptoms of complacency. All growth curves have a lifeline, both in your personal and professional life. Personal relationships often stall and falter because couples aren't purposeful enough about taking things to the next curve, such as new adventures, new people, new jobs, different cities. Complacency definitely can take its toll on relationships. People stall professionally too, staying in roles that hardly invigorate or stretch them anymore, only to find themselves as headcount in the inevitable cycle of restructures. To grow yourself and the team, you must be comfortable with discomfort. It is indeed a paradox in life, the inherent tension between comfort and discomfort, best described in Charles Handy's classic, *The Age of Paradox*.

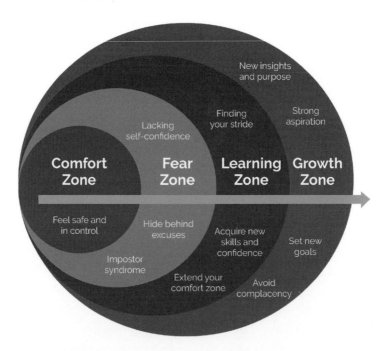

There are four zones associated with personal stretch and growth. As a leader and coach, it helps to know the four zones and the ramifications for being in each.

The first is the *comfort zone*, the one that most people have to push themselves out of with conscious purpose. Aspiration certainly helps, that desire to grow your capability and confidence to have greater impact in life. Some people thrive on stretching themselves, which reflects a bias for and comfort with disruption. A reminder here that boredom is a major stressor in life, albeit subliminal, so most people do have to be pushed or pulled out of their comfort zone. Empathy helps in a major way when you tap a person on the shoulder and suggest they may be ready for a stretch in their life. It is conveyed through knowing what it feels like to be terrified when someone believes in you before you do. When you push someone out of their comfort zone, stay close to them to help normalise the fear that comes with being stretched onto a new curve.

Just outside the comfort zone is the *fear zone*, which is a common and natural response when people are pushed into the realm of uncertainty. The fear zone is ripe with the essential ingredients for impostor syndrome. When people are asked to stretch themselves, it is natural for them to doubt their abilities, sometimes to withdraw inward where they seem detached and difficult to connect with. Or they puff up into Third Circle, like a blowfish. In either scenario, this is when empathy really matters. Your role as a coach is to keep them talking, to pull their perspective outward and provide positive reinforcement for progress they might not see in themselves. This is when the power of a personal story can really make a difference for the person, where they hear through your own experience the clear parallels to what they are going through. A personal story about having gone through a similar experience is a great way to convey empathy.

> *Empathy helps in a major way when you tap a person on the shoulder and suggest they may be ready for a stretch in their life.*

The *learning zone* follows the fear zone, where you push beyond the anxiety, self-doubt and apprehensions about your own capability. You can perhaps relate to those emotions from your own experiences with personal or career stretch, where you start to gain a bit of traction and your confidence kicks in. We have all been on learning curves, dozens of times in our lives. It is literally like climbing a hill, the first couple of weeks feeling very steep where you try to lock into pace, followed by a sense of traction where your focus is less on whether you can do it and more on the destination ahead. It is helpful for people to hear how they are succeeding in a new role and exactly where they have made a difference. It comes back to the power of positive reinforcement that fuels the human need for esteem. Fuelling people for where they have done well is so much more effective than constantly focusing on their mistakes and errors. To be fair, you have to do both. But people give you far more latitude to focus on their mistakes if they believe you really value them in the first instance. A great example of compassionate empathy is you making the time to fuel a person who is on a steep learning curve, to reinforce their traction and impact. Your positivity and optimism make a big difference.

The final zone is all about *growth*, where you have learned some new skills or ways of thinking and then start to apply them. Most people can relate to the growth zone when reflecting back on when they first learned to drive a car. You remember the excitement when you were officially deemed a 'legitimate' driver, when you no longer had the 'L' in the back window. The fear zone would be the anxiety you felt the very first time you sat behind the wheel, maybe even reluctant to turn the key. The learning zone would be your first few drives with your mum or dad, who were there to train you. And the growth zone would be your very cocky stride to the car the moment after you earned your license with no restrictions. For most people, reflecting back on that moment is a perfect example of how the human need for esteem is typically met through some source of validation, whether official or unofficial. As a leader, your validation of a person's growth carries a lot of weight. Talk regularly with members of your team about where you have seen growth in their capability and confidence. That way, they can begin to fine-tune the nuances to have maximum impact.

A great example of compassionate empathy is you making the time to fuel a person who is on a steep learning curve, to reinforce their traction and impact.

Trust Your Intuition. As a leader, it is not just about making empathy real for your team. It's also about making empathy right, which often requires a shift in mindset for some people who will evolve over time. That shift in mindset has been accelerated by more focus on engagement in organisations. The research is compelling when drawing a direct correlation between staff engagement and results. To be clear, the right brain now has equal impact with the left brain in terms of how people, particularly senior leaders, are appraised on their annual performance reviews. That was not the case 20 years ago when technical and functional expertise was the big ticket to career progression. Now, well into the twenty-first century, and true to Goleman's prediction, we know that you will not progress as a leader without a decent degree of emotional intelligence.

Intuition resides within the right brain. Encourage yourself and anyone you are coaching to listen closely to a particular feeling they may have, even if there is nothing rational to explain it, such as when giving a presentation and you sense most people have detached. You don't know this for sure, but you can 'feel' it. In this example, rather than ploughing through the next 25 slides as you had originally planned, you might step away from the presentation and ask what would be of most interest to the group in the remaining 20 minutes. Watch the immediate impact that question has on the energy level in the room. When you invite people into your thinking and the conversation, it enhances connection. Empathy is about knowing how and when to enhance connection in a genuine way. Learn to give your right brain more say in how you land on a particular decision. Listen to your intuition when it speaks to you; it is likely signalling for you to show some empathy.

18

FINAL WRAP

Head, Heart and Hands. That is all you need to encode from the many pages leading up to these final words. Empathy is all about understanding, feeling and doing. For each of us, this powerful trio has made a huge difference in our ability to push through any challenge or to help others to do so. To know and show empathy, practise the rule of three as often as you can.

Em-pa-thy

People like being understood rather than judged. The connection comes from you listening with interest rather than judgement, even if your final decision differs from what they would have preferred. They are more likely to follow you if they believe you have heard them. That feeling of being heard and understood is largely intuitive. People know when you are not listening to them to learn, but instead to refute what they have said. Make more effort to understand where the other person is coming from. Active listening means you are really listening.

People like it when they know you have once felt what they feel, perhaps even gone through something together, like COVID-19. And they don't need you to tell them how they should feel or why they shouldn't feel a particular way. They just need to know you can relate viscerally to what they are going through at the moment. It might mean crying with someone or even praying with someone, or just being fully present as they talk about something going on with them. There is power in the sentiment behind a 'heartfelt connection'.

Actions really do speak louder than words. Pick up the phone and call someone to ask about their ailing parent or child. Drop in on a peer at work to tell them what you really liked about their presentation earlier that day, especially what you learned from it. Invite a team member for a coffee and ask about their experience with a particular challenge you are now facing and what advice they would offer. Give a person a day off to sort through some stuff going on in their lives, especially if they have consistently gone the extra mile for the business. Take the pressure off yourself to be all-knowing and invite people into your thinking.

EM-PA-THY: It is time to make it real for leaders, now more so than ever before. In a post-COVID world in which change will swirl even faster, we must be more attuned to what will enable people to thrive. Daniel Goleman was spot-on with his prediction. EQ is now the deal breaker with empathy at its core. Try to understand people better. Imagine walking in their shoes. It also helps to feel another person's pain — not to wear it, but to know what it feels like. And compassion is as human as it gets. Short and sweet, empathy is all about being there.

REFERENCES
AND RESOURCES

Atlassian. Retrieved from https://www.atlassian.com/blog/archives/
collaboration-best-practices-3-reasons-interruptions-hurt-
productivity

Blanchard, K. (2012). Collaboration — Affect/Possibility. Retrieved
from https://www.youtube.com/watch?v=HKGkBRk1kSo

Bregman, P. (2010). How (and Why) to Stop Multitasking. *Harvard
Business Review*. Retrieved from https://hbr.org/2010/05/how-
and-why-to-stop-multi-tasking

Brown, B. (2010). The Power of Vulnerability. Retrieved from
https://www.ted.com/talks/brene_brown_the_power_of_
vulnerability?language=en

Center for Creative Leadership. (2020). The Importance of Empathy
in the Workplace. Retrieved from https://www.ccl.org/articles/
leading-effectively-articles/empathy-in-the-workplace-a-tool-for-
effective-leadership/

Davis, D. (2017). Klan We Talk. Retrieved from https://www.ted.com/
talks/daryl_davis_klan_we_talk

Goleman, D. (1995). *Emotional Intelligence*. Bantam Books, Inc.

Handy, C. B. (1994). *The Age of Paradox*. Harvard Business School
Press.

Hillman, H. (2015). *Fitting In, Standing Out*. Penguin Random House
New Zealand.

Hillman, H. (2013). *The Impostor Syndrome*. Random House New Zealand.

Maslow, A. H. (1943). A Theory of Human Motivation. *Psychological Review,* 50(4), 370–396. https://doi.org/10.1037/h005436

Ovans, A. (2015). What Resilience Is, And Why It Matters. *Harvard Business Review*. Retrieved from https://hbr.org/2015/01/what-resilience-means-and-why-it-matters

Rodenburg, P. (2008). *The Second Circle: Using Positive Energy for Success in Every Situation*. W.W. Norton.